Occupational
Ethics Series

Elizabeth Beardsley and John Atwell,
Series Editors

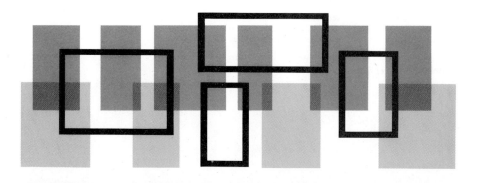

Ethics in Policy Analysis

ROSEMARIE TONG
Williams College

PRENTICE-HALL, INC. Englewood Cliffs, New Jersey 07632

Library of Congress Cataloging-in-Publication Data

Tong, Rosemarie.
  Ethics in policy analysis.

  (Occupational ethics series)
  Includes bibliographies and index.
  1. Policy sciences—Moral and ethical aspects.
I. Title. II. Series.
H97.T66 1986   174'.936161   85-12391
ISBN 0-13-290917-0

Editorial/production supervision: Cyndy Lyle Rymer
Manufacturing buyer: Harry P. Baisley

Printed in the United States of America

10 9 8 7 6 5 4 3 2 1

ISBN 0-13-290917-0 01

Prentice-Hall International (UK) Limited, *London*
Prentice-Hall of Australia Pty. Limited, *Sydney*
Prentice-Hall Canada Inc., *Toronto*
Prentice-Hall Hispanoamericana, S.A., *Mexico*
Prentice-Hall of India Private Limited, *New Delhi*
Prentice-Hall of Japan, Inc., *Tokyo*
Prentice-Hall of Southeast Asia Pte. Ltd., *Singapore*
Editora Prentice-Hall do Brasil, Ltda., *Rio de Janeiro*
Whitehall Books Limited, *Wellington, New Zealand*

To the four men in my life:

Joseph John Behensky, my father
Paul Ki-king Tong, my husband
Paul Shih-Mien Tong, my first-born
John Shih-Chiung Tong, my second-born

Contents

Prentice-Hall Series in Occupational Ethics

An increasing number of philosophers are coming to appreciate the value of making our discipline constructively available to those whose lives are chiefly focused on some form of practical activity. It is natural that philosophers specializing in ethics should be in the forefront of this movement toward "applied philosophy." In both writing and teaching many leading ethical theorists are currently dealing with concrete issues in individual and social life.

While this change has been taking place within the philosophic community, practitioners in various fields have (for several complex reasons) turned their attention to the ethical dimensions of their own activities. Whether they work in areas traditionally called "professions" or in other occupations, they wish to consider their job-related decisions in relation to ethical principles and social goals. They rightly recognize that many, if not most, ethical problems facing all of us arise in our occupational lives: we are often expected to conduct ourselves "at work" in ways which appear to conflict with the ethical principles believed valid in other social relationships; in our occupations themselves certain normally accepted practices sometimes seem to contradict each other; in short, ethical dilemmas of enormous proportion face the morally conscientious person. Whether philosophical ethics can help resolve these acute problems is an inescapable question.

A third recent development is the growing tendency of students to think of themselves as persons who do or will have certain occupational roles. This tendency is noticeable at several stages of life—in choosing an occupation, in preparing for one already chosen, and in pursuing one that has been entered some time ago.

The convergence of these three contemporary developments has created a need for appropriate teaching materials. The *Occupational Ethics* Series is designed to meet this need. Each volume has been written by a philosopher, with the advice or collaboration of a practitioner in a particular occupation. The volumes are suitable for liberal arts courses in ethics and for programs of preprofessional study, as well as for the general reader who seeks a better understanding of a world that most human beings inhabit, the world of work.

John E. Atwell and Elizabeth L. Beardsley, Editors

Preface

In recent years philosophers have sought to construct diverse ethical systems for professionals. Numerous books and articles have been written about medical, legal, and business ethics. By way of contrast, relatively few works have had as their main focus the ethics of professions like architecture, dentistry, the ministry, computer programming, teaching, and nursing. This volume probes the moral dimensions of a cluster of professions that have only recently become self-consciously aware of themselves as professionals; namely, the related professions of policy analyzing, advising, and consulting. I became interested in these budding professions as a result of teaching a course entitled "Moral Dimensions of Public Policy" for Williams College's Political-Economy Program. A month or two into the course, I realized that the literature paid only passing obesance to the ethics of expertise. I would skim through book after book on public policy to find either no mention of ethics or a few cursory pages devoted to it. Given that so many of my students were planning careers as policy experts, I regretted this absence of ethical discussion and decided to do something about it. After consulting several Williams' graduates, who had gone on to policy jobs in Washington, D.C., I formulated a tentative outline for *Ethics in Policy Analysis*. Thanks to the comments and criticisms of these alumni, the book that greets you today is far better than the book that would have greeted you a year or two ago. There is no better corrective for the heady idealism of the armchair philosopher than the commonsense realism of those who practice the professions he or she seeks to analyze.

Before introducing the main topics of this book in some depth and at some length, I would like to summarize them quickly, chapter by chapter. Chapter One employs a case study to orientate wary readers as they set sail through the uncharted waters of ethics for policy experts. Chapter Two deals with the epistemological problems likely to confront the policy expert. In the main these problems have to do with the relation between either fact and value or knowledge and belief. If anything has become clear to contemporary policy experts, it is that their numbers, statistics, polls, and studies are admixtures of objective fact and subjective value, and that the whole truth and nothing but the truth is simply unavailable to them. Chapter Three probes the legitimate role of the expert in a democracy, analyzing the relationship between knowledge (in the person of the policy expert) and power (in the person of the policymaker). A concerted effort is also made to address both the reasons that justify and the causes that explain citizen activism on the one hand and citizen apathy on the other. Chapter Four discusses the ways in which the structures of a bureaucracy can either facilitate or impede ascriptions of personal responsibility. Any serious study of ethics in policy analysis cannot afford to neglect the fact that policy experts work not in vacuums but in institutions that operate according to their own rhyme and reason. Chapter Five is devoted to a search for that approach to the moral life which will best enable the policy expert to be a good person and to perform the right action. The ethics of virtue or character is both compared and contrasted with the ethics of rules or principles before both approaches are combined. Chapters Six and Seven focus not only on the specific obligations policy experts have to their clients and to third parties respectively, but also on the array of virtues policy experts ought to cultivate in their quest for an excellent public as well as personal life.

Although this book merely touches upon the issues and ideas that influence the moral selves and moral actions of policy analysts, advisers, and consultants, it does provide a foundation upon which other moral philosophers and policy experts can build. Those who read this book will doubtlessly find many more interesting and important things to say about ethics in policy analysis. Should this happen, I will be most pleased. For now, I rest content to have played a part in articulating an ethics for at least some of my students.

Chapter 1

Introduction

CASE STUDY: DAVID STOCKMAN
AND "REAGONOMICS"

When David Stockman, director of the Office of Management and Budget, publicly admitted that "None of us really understands what's going on with all these numbers,"[1] we were reminded that policy decisions often flow from figures that are far from conclusive. In large measure, public policy is shaped away from common public knowledge, by experts who have been called upon to manage diverse, numerous, and ambiguous factors. To be sure, the policy expert is not a new invention. Experts of one sort or another have existed as long as humans have lived in society, and they have always claimed that they have special knowledge beyond the ken of ordinary citizens. As George Kelly has put it, policy experts have played a constant role in history, "wearing among other transitory costumes, those of the musician, tax-collector, confessor, constitution-writer, strategist, and economic planner," and "pronouncing anathemas and justifications" that may serve the populace well but are beyond their full comprehension.[2]

Today the policy expert usually appears in the guise of an analyst, adviser, subject-area specialist, or consultant, and he or she is likely to be found in almost any government agency that can afford its own stationery. The number of policy experts is increasing at such a rate that Daniel Guttman and Barry Wilner, coauthors of *The Shadow Government: The Government's Multi-Billion Dollar Giveaway of Its Decision-Making Powers to Private Management Consultants, "Experts," and Think Tanks*, tell us that policy analysis is the largest industry in the nation's capital. A 1979 edition of the Washington, D.C., Yellow Pages listed about 120 economic and social researchers, 150 educational researchers, 400 management consultants, and 15 urban affairs consultants, to say nothing of the hundreds of

1

other policy experts, even more specialized, that graced its pages.[3] In a similar vein, a recent issue of *Society* devoted all its pages to a discussion of the "Policy Analysis Explosion," documenting the exponential growth of this new field during the past decade. Currently, the federal government alone spends between $500 million and $1 billion annually for policy analysis (depending on what one includes under that term), and there is every indication that these expenditures will continue to grow.[4]

As policymakers become more dependent on policy experts for information and advice, we become increasingly concerned about the character and conduct of these experts. A case in point is that of David Stockman, President Reagan's chief economist during his 1980–84 term of office. In a lengthy *Atlantic Monthly* article, William Greider reports that Stockman was hired early in 1980 to demonstrate that the nation could prosper under "Reaganomics."[5] Eager to prove themselves, Stockman and his Office of Management and Budget (OMB) staff instructed their computer to calculate the economic impact of Reagan's plan to decrease taxation while increasing defense spending. The computer was not encouraging. It predicted that if Reagan went ahead with his plans, the federal budget would face a series of unprecedented deficits ranging from $82 billion in 1982 to $116 billion in 1984. Curiously, Stockman saw not impending doom but a golden opportunity in these projections—the opportunity to debunk such conventional premises as continuing double-digit inflation and persistent patterns of slow economic growth, and to forward in their stead such unconventional assumptions as plummeting interest rates and rapid economic growth. Stockman used these radical assumptions about the economy to reprogram the OMB computer, which then proceeded to spew out more reassuring projections than it had originally produced. Provided that the President realized that more than mismanagement, fraud, and waste would have to be eliminated to achieve a balanced budget,[6] all would be well.

Apparently convinced by his adviser's arguments, President Reagan instructed Stockman to make the necessary cuts—about $40 billion dollars worth. In his search for monetary excesses, Stockman scrutinized the four major parts of the budget. He noted that 48 cents of the federal dollar went to Social Security, Medicare, veteran benefits, and the like; that 25 cents belonged to the Pentagon for national defense; that 10 cents was targeted to interest payments on the national debt; and that 17 cents covered government operations (highways, parks, weather bureaus, etc.), welfare projects, and grants-in-aid. Since Reagan initially refused to touch the first three parts of the budget, Stockman realized that he would have to make the needed cuts from the fourth part of the budget, a part of the budget near and dear to the hearts of Cabinet members. Appealing to team spirit, Stockman urged Cabinet members either to eliminate any nonessential program or to reduce it substantially. At first Stockman's strategy worked. Cabinet members succumbed to peer pressure and parted with their pet park, highway, dam, and welfare programs in their mutual pursuit of the common good. Encouraged by these voluntary relinquishments, Stockman proposed to cut $752 million from the Export-Import Bank, which provides subsidized financing for international trade. Apparently, Stockman's attack on Ex-Im was motivated by his desire to make things "look right." After all, how could he cut food stamps, social services, CETA and EDA jobs without making any dents in the coffers of the wealthy? Largely because of President Reagan's unexpected opposition, however, Stockman lost not only the Ex-Im battle but also the battle to close the tax "loopholes" benefiting big business interests. Rather than faulting Reagan for his resistance, the resilient Stockman simply stated that he did not really need to deprive either Ex-Im of its subsidies or big business of its profits to make the economy thrive. Such proposals were mere "equity ornaments" inessential to the "economics of the thing."[7]

Despite his failure to secure as many dollars from the rich as from the poor, Stockman negotiated the rest of his cuts through Congress. A person of considerable charm and eloquence, Stockman took care of Senators' and Representatives' "embarrassing questions about future deficits" with a wave of his "magic asterisk," a punctuation mark that promised to turn red into black.[8] Nevertheless, despite his ability to convince almost everybody that the budget was salvageable, Stockman could not defend himself against his own growing doubts about its soundness. In no uncertain terms, Stockman told the administration that if it wished to survive, it would have to attack its three sacred cows: defense, Social Security, and Medicare/Medicaid. Reluctantly, the White House agreed to take a large bite out of Social Security, proposing a drastic reduction in benefits for those who wished to retire at 62. Congress reacted negatively to the proposal. Faced with a major political uproar, Stockman admitted that his proposal had "a lot of technical bloopers" because he had written it under unfavorable time constraints. Said Stockman, "I was just racing against the clock. All the office things I knew ought to be done by way of groundwork, advance preparation, and so forth just fell by the wayside. . ."[9] Nevertheless, Stockman believed that after Congress recovered from the initial shock of his proposal, it would allow him to take a few nibbles out of Social Security's hide. As it turned out, Stockman was not allowed to chew this piece of fat. None other than President Reagan disavowed the OMB director's plans for Social Security.

Blocked by Reagan and faced with some very real deficits, Stockman proceeded to outline a more modest tax-cut policy than the one President Reagan had initially announced to the nation. At first the Republican White House agreed to these smaller tax cuts, only to retreat later, when the Democrats enlarged their tax-cut proposal. The administration's vacillation on the tax bill ushered in a six-week period of lobbying, during which Stockman promised to return a measure of the funds he had taken away from various departments and agencies. He promised to earmark millions more for Medicaid, home-heating subsidies, mass-transit operating funds, and other popular programs and projects. But even though Stockman made these conciliatory gestures in public, in private he stated that some of these "final" figures were mere "authorization ceilings" that could be whittled down later.[10] Even though Stockman's seeming duplicity bothered Congress, it ultimately endorsed a budget reduction of $35.1 billion. Thus, in political terms Stockman had achieved a victory. Nevertheless, he began to worry about the "wonder" he had wrought, expressing concern both about the means he had employed to effect it and about the ends he had come to serve. Indeed, what came to trouble Stockman most, speculates William Greider, was the realization that when push came to shove, "the 'idea-based' policies that he had espoused at the outset were . . . greately compromised by the 'constituency-based' politics that he abhorred."[11] Although Stockman continued to serve as OMB director, he was, by his own admission, not the same man Reagan had hired in 1980. Stockman the indomitable idealist was no more. In his place stood Stockman the quintessential realist.

INTERPRETATION AND ANALYSIS
OF THE STOCKMAN CASE

Several features of Stockman's case are particularly instructive, and each of them will be discussed at length in subsequent chapters. Chapter 2, "Ethics, Epistemology, and the Expert," underlines the extent to which irrationalities and inefficiencies infect the policymaking process and the degree to which values shape facts. Natural and social scientists were invited to join the government in large numbers during the 1960s because they promised to interject not only analytic rhyme but disciplined reason into the vagaries of policymaking. Science was going to supplant politics. The techniques of operations research, systems analysis, cost-effectiveness analysis, cost-benefit analysis, and risk-benefit analysis were going to replace the tactics of wheeling and dealing, logrolling, pork barreling, and general lobbying. Neutral facts were to supplant biased values. Henceforward, rationality and efficiency rather than passion and waste were to order our civil lives. As usual, however, mind did not triumph entirely over matter. Policy experts soon confronted the limits of their abilities. If David Stockman, for example, learned anything in Washington, D.C., it was that policy analyzing, advising, and consulting is frequently anything but neutral, rational, and efficient. And if we learned anything from David Stockman, it was that even the best and the brightest of experts can, in relatively good conscience, adopt a biased *modus operandi*. When Stockman changed the OMB's computer program, he saw nothing untoward in his decision to assume both a swift decline in prices and interest rates and a dramatic surge in productivity. It did not bother him that other economists were assuming precisely the opposite, namely, double-digit inflation and slow economic growth. Despite this fundamental disagreement, Stockman simply claimed that his preferred economic paradigm, the radical supply-side paradigm, was just as "valid" as any competing economic paradigm:

> It's based on valid economic analysis . . . but it's the inverse of the last four years. When we go public, this is going to set off a wide-open debate on how the economy works, a great battle over the conventional theories of economic performance.[12]

But even if there is nothing unseemly about adversarial economics, one may wonder whether Stockman's choice of economic paradigm was motivated purely by epistemological considerations or at least partially by political commitments to Ronald Reagan.

This last question is probably unanswerable, but questions like it—as well as questions about the supposed rationality, objectivity, and neutrality of science—are leading policy experts to describe policy analysis, advising, and consulting as arts rather than sciences. Aaron Wildavsky is convinced, for example, that policy analysis is an art based on the creative and imaginative use of limited information to explore policy possibilities. It is necessarily an art rather than a science because:

> The technical base of policy analysis is weak. In part its limitations are those of social science's innumerable discrete propositions of varying validity and uncertain applicability, occasionally touching but not necessarily related, like beads on a string. Its strengths lie in the ability to make a little knowledge go a long way by combining an understanding of the constraints of the situation with the ability to explore the environment constructively.[13]

Although many policy experts still maintain that the policy sciences are rigorous sciences (at least in their potentialities if not in their actualities), an equal number are ready to concede with Aristotle that, like ethics, policy science can yield only partial and provisional truths. Thus, Chapter 2 examines the shift away from the "value-free" epistemology of the old positivist tradition to the "value-laden" epistemology of the new "interpretive" tradition. It also considers the moral problems generated by the standard techniques of the policy sciences: operations research, systems analysis, cost-effectiveness analysis, cost-benefit analysis, and risk-benefit analysis. Finally, it touches upon the sensitive relationship among one's epistemology, politics, and ethics, discussing the extent to which values and facts are interwoven.

Another point the Stockman case brings to focus, and one that is highlighted in Chapter 3, "The Role of the Expert in a Democratic Society," is the crucial role analysts, advisers, and consultants can and do often play in the shaping of public policy. Faced with a multibillion-dollar deficit, Stockman and his team began to thin out the budget. As the pruning process proceeded, it became clear that policy-makers were relying on him and the OMB team to make all sorts of decisions for them. The order to cut $40 billion dollars from the budget was carried out by Stockman largely as he saw fit.

> I put together a list of twenty social programs that have to be zeroed out completely, like Job Corps, Head Start, women and children's feeding programs, on and on. And another twenty-five that have to be cut by 50 percent: general revenue sharing, CETA manpower training, etcetera, etcetera. And then huge bites that would have to be taken out of Social Security. I mean really fierce blood-and-guts stuff—widows' benefits and orphans' benefits, things like that.[14]

But, we may wonder, why should a "whiz kid" like David Stockman have so much "in-put" in important decisions? And why should policy experts set the terms of discourse for policymakers, determining the conceptual parameters within which policy decisions are made? Were policy experts few in number, these questions would not be so pressing; but today scores of analysts, advisers, and consultants help legislators, executives, and members of the judiciary forge public policy. Like it or not, we rely on political scientists, economists, sociologists, psychologists, anthropologists, physicists, biochemists, mathematicians, computer scientists, engineers, and more for assurance that the costs of living in society will not outweigh its benefits. And like it or not, the way in which these experts make their services available to us can significantly affect the distribution of political power in our society. If policy scientists give government and industry the exclusive benefit of their expertise, they may inadvertently contribute to the creation of a technocracy in which we must accept whatever Big Brother or Big Sister tells us is in our interest. If, however, these scientists make available to us the information we need for the maintenance and enhancement of our lives and liberties, they can help effect a more participatory mode of decision making.

Given, then, that policy experts can contribute either to democracy's expansion or erosion, Chapter 3 discusses the growing power of policy experts, and whether it should be curbed or expanded. Those who favor *less* powerful experts have raised three objections: (1) *the cultural objection*—the position that the historical process which resulted in the subordination first of ethical discourse and then of democratic political discourse to the technological discourse of policy experts is deleterious and dangerous for the human community; (2) *the political objection*—the charge that policy experts and policymakers have such a monopoly on power that the voice of the people is effectively silenced; and (3) *the ethical objection*—the view that the increasing hegemony of policy experts demoralizes the populace at large either by contributing to the typical citizen's sense of ignorance and powerlessness or by eroding the citizen's desire to make decisions or to take an active role in the policy process. In response to these objections, those who favor more powerful experts have made three replies: (1) Many citizens are neither able nor willing to participate in the policy process; (2) some of the citizens who are most willing to participate in the policy process are the least able in that they lack adequate knowledge; and (3) some of the citizens who are most able to participate in the policy process are the least willing in that they lack adequate time, energy, or motivation. Chapter 3 sorts through all these objections and replies. It argues not so much against powerful policy experts as in favor of a well-informed citizenry, actively engaged in the policy process. In a democratic, pluralistic society, ethics and politics progress by means of what Alasdair MacIntyre describes as a mutual search, largely conversational, for the human good.[15] Thus, to exclude the citizenry from policy discussion is both to subvert the democratic process and to erode moral dialogue. Whatever else policy experts do, therefore, they should advocate citizen participation. Citizens are, relatively speaking, limited in specialized knowledge and in power, but this does not mean that they cannot or should not make their will felt about policy decisions. Indeed, designing policies that facilitate intelligent and effective citizen participation must be an essential task of policy experts.

The fourth point the Stockman case highlights, and one that is underscored in Chapter 4, "The Policy Expert within the Bureaucracy's Bowels," is the way in which bureaucratic structures tend to defeat ascriptions of responsibility and to deaden moral sensibilities. Depending on the complexity of the bureaucracy in which they work, policy experts may feel that their decisions are made for them, that they are responsible for too little ("I'm only a cog in a machine") or that they are responsible for too much ("We are part of all that we have met"). Looking back at his team's efforts to balance the budget, Stockman confessed to William Greider that

> ... the defense numbers got out of control and we were doing that whole budget-cutting exercise so frenetically. In other words, you were juggling details, pushing people, and going from one session to another, trying to cut housing programs here and rural electric there, and we were doing it so fast, we didn't know where we were ending up for sure. . . . And it didn't quite mesh.[16]

But even though not only Stockman but President Reagan knew that Reaganomics was not working, Stockman and his OMB team remained silent as the President proceeded to tell the American people that all was well.

Although we can only speculate about the motivations grounding the silence of Stockman *et al.*, some of the OMB team may have kept quiet for fear of antagonizing the President. Others may have held their peace for fear of alarming the public unnecessarily. By stalling for time, the analysts could juggle the numbers until the President's overly optimistic words rang true. Thus, Chapter 4 explores the ways in which bureaucratic structures and pressures affect the moral psychology of the policy expert. It describes those features of the bureaucratic environment most likely to weaken moral resolve—the pressure to conform to organizational norms, to join in the general scramble for prestige and power, and to manipulate people (and, in worst-case situations, one's data and analysis) in order to gain access to those empowered to make the decisions. This is part of the general bureaucratic structure, where "knowledge" speaks to "power," and where experts must of necessity concern themselves with gaining access to powerful policymakers if they are to have any assurance that their studies or reports will do more than gather dust in a file cabinet. In addition, the desire for influence and access to power may lead to an analyst's, adviser's, or consultant's becoming a mere "hired brain," gearing analysis and conclusions toward the prejudices of the policymakers. Bureaucratic pressures such as these often turn the analyst into a supporter by default of the status quo or the latest political trend.

Chapter 4 also focuses on the so-called "dirty hands" justification and the so-called "many hands" excuse. It is argued by some that because policy experts are operating in the *public* realm on behalf of the common good, they may be either permitted or required to act in ways that would be wrong in *private* life. If so, we cannot blame Stockman and the OMB team for telling a few half-truths and whole lies in the short run in order to achieve a sound economy in the long run. Similarly, it is argued by others, that because so many policy experts and policymakers contribute to government decisions, it is difficult in principle to identify who is morally responsible for a given policy decision. If so, we cannot blame Stockman and the OMB team for the state of the economy. Their hands were not the only ones stirring the budgetary brew, and the spices they added to the economic soup may not have been the ones that ultimately determined its objectionable flavor. After articulating both the weaknesses and the strengths of these arguments, Chapter 4 forwards a hands-on model of personal responsibility, according to which policy experts are accountable for all their voluntary actions. To the degree that policy experts act in knowledge and with power, to that same degree they cannot escape either praise or blame for their actions.

The fifth and perhaps most important point the Stockman case highlights, and one to which Chapter 5, "Towards an Ethics for Policy Experts," is devoted, is the extent to which ethical questions—even if they are ignored or trivialized—are implicated in policy considerations. "Equity ornaments" (to use Stockman's term) decorate every policy expert's Christmas tree, and whether he or she discounts them as mere baubles or treasures them as crowning glories depends more on the expert's implicit or explicit frame of values than on his or her technical skills. It has been convincingly argued that unless policy experts confront the moral dimensions of their occupation squarely, they cannot act in the public's best interest. Policy analysts, for example, cannot study health-care policy adequately without confronting the crucial issues of who should get health care, how, when, and why. Nor can science advisers study nuclear energy and arms policy thoroughly without facing the central issue of the value of life. To pretend otherwise is to construct a public policy that is at best superficial and at worst hostile to whatever separates beasts from human persons.

If ethics is to become an integral part of the policymaking process, then students of public policy must excel in moral reasoning as well as political know-how and technical skill. Many policy experts and citizens do indeed want to include ethics in the public-policy curriculum, but not every professor or student shares this enthusiasm. Some educators, for example, believe that ethical judgments are not amenable to rational analysis and as such have no place in the academic forum. The source of this view is the positivist assumption that separates fact from value, descriptive statements from evaluative statements. Because descriptive statements—such as "It will cost $3,000,000 to remove the toxic waste from this canal"—are subject to empirical vertification, whereas evaluative statements—such as "The health of ten persons is more important than saving ten industrialists $300,000 apiece"—are not, positivists argue that only descriptive statements are amenable to rational discourse. This being the supposed case, positivists conclude that if policy experts wish to characterize their contribution to the policymaking process as one that rescues public policy from the emotive snares of personal preference, arbitrary whim, and mindless caprice, then they must take care to remain in the realm of fact, guarding against the realm of value and its forbidden fruit: ethics.

What is amazing about this dichotomous world view is that it has held sway for so long. Upon reflection, it seems clear that ethical judgments are not the product of lonely subjectivity, they are predominantly interpersonal positions supported by reasons. We all make intuitive distinctions between expressions of preference and expressions of moral judgment. When someone professes that they prefer raspberry yogurt to all other flavors of yogurt, I will probably note my passion for cherry yogurt and leave it at that. But should someone announce, "Murder is right," I will both demand reasons for such a claim and state my reasons for thinking that murder is wrong. We debate matters of the latter sort and not of the former precisely because we presuppose that moral judgments, unlike emotive utterances, are amenable to rational discourse. Actually, we presuppose more than this. We also believe that moral discourse is guided by a set of criteria according to which our respective moral points of view can be ranked as better or worse. Many believe that these criteria are, in some sense of the term, "utilitarian," or related to our concern with the distribution of pleasure (benefits) and pain (burdens) among the human community. Others believe that these criteria have less to do with utilitarian considerations than with ideas like "treating others as you would like to be treated in comparable circumstances," "judging the morality of principles by the consequences of their universal application," and minimizing "fortuitous human differences" as a basis for differential treatment.[17] In any event, no matter what we identify as the criteria for rightness and wrongness, it is possible to distinguish a moral *reason* for action from a personal *cause* of action, a rational justification from a psychological explanation.

But even if we agree that evaluative statements are amenable to rational discourse, it would be a mistake to conclude that ethics is simply a matter of first determining a set of rational rules for conduct and then following them no matter what. Ethics is as much about virtues as it is about rules, about character as it is about conduct. Chapter 5 argues that if policy analysts, advisers, and consultants are to develop as moral agents, then they must have a conception of themselves as virtuous persons as well as a conception of themselves as rule abiders. If a person is not interested in developing his moral character, probably he will not care about articulating and following justified moral rules. Similarly, if a person does not care about moral rules, most likely he will not be interested in moral character.

Building on the central insight of Chapter 5—namely, that ethics is both a matter of developing character and following rules—Chapters 6 and 7 respectively will focus on the remaining point the Stockman case raises: namely, how the professional obligations of political experts to their clients—honesty, candor, competence, diligence, loyalty, and discretion[18]—can and do come into conflict with their ordinary obligations to third parties—justice and benevolence.[19] For example, in his desire to remain loyal to President Reagan, David Stockman stood silently by as the chief executive painted a beautiful picture of an ugly economy. By so doing, Stockman deprived a very large third party—the American people—of information that may have been crucial to their well-being. Such conflicts are by no means rare, and the conscientious policy expert wants to know what he or she ought to do when confronted with a moral dilemma. Is resignation, whistle blowing, or "leaking" in order? In an effort to answer this and related questions, Chapters 6 and 7 discuss what the ethics of conduct and the ethics of character offer policy experts in the way of moral guidance on routine days at the office as well as during those dark nights when multiple duties, rights, and virtues war against each other.

Whatever else this book accomplishes, its overall aim is to provide policy experts and the public with a vision of policy analyzing, advising, and consulting as practices. According to philosopher Alasdair MacIntyre, a practice is a cooperative human activity which has its own internal standards of excellence.[20] The pursuit of the natural and social sciences, the art of politics, doctoring, teaching, lawyering, parenting, and yes, policy analyzing, advising, and consulting are all practices. Sometimes these practices serve goods external to themselves, as when one engages in policy analysis for prestige or in consulting for money; but they require for their well-being an appreciation of those goods that are internal to the practice. Try, for example, to imagine a great teacher who was motivated only by money and prestige. The imagination resists precisely because such a teacher, however competent, would not be "great." In order to be great, teachers have to treasure what they do simply because doing it as well as possible makes them better persons. Becoming a moral person is a lifelong task, but this task is what gives meaning to one's professional as well as personal life. Absent this quest, policy analysis would not be a practice but a mere technical skill better performed by computers; and, absent this quest, there would be no need for a book entitled *Ethics in Policy Analysis.*

NOTES

1. William Greider, "The Education of David Stockman," *Atlantic Monthly* (December 1981): 38.

2. Arnold J. Meltsner, *Policy Analysis in the Bureaucracy* (Berkeley and Los Angeles: University of California Press, 1976), 51–52.

3. Edward W. Lehman, "Policy Mix and the Quality of Information," *Society* 16, no. 6 (September/October 1979), 38.

4. Alice M. Rivlin, *Systematic Thinking for Social Action* (Washington, D.C.: Brookings Institution, 1971).

5. The David Stockman case study presented here is based on William Greider's lengthly *Atlantic Monthly* interview with Stockman. For the full account, see Greider, "The Education of David Stockman," 27–54.

6. Greider, "The Education of David Stockman," 52.

7. Ibid., 36.

8. Ibid., 39.

9. Ibid., 45.

10. Ibid., 50.

11. Ibid., 32.

12. Ibid.

13. Aaron Wildavsky, *Speaking Truth to Power: The Art and Craft of Policy Analysis* (Boston: Little, Brown and Company, 1979) 15.

14. Greider, "The Education of David Stockman," 40.

15. Alasdair MacIntyre, *After Virtue* (Notre Dame, Ind.: University of Notre Dame Press, 1979), 169–89.

16. Greider, "The Education of David Stockman," 40.

17. David A. J. Richards, *The Moral Criticism of Law* (Encino and Belmont, Calif.: Dickenson Publishing Company, Inc., 1977), 105.

18. Michael D. Bayles, *Professional Ethics* (Belmont, Calif.: Wadsworth Publishing Co., 1981), 70–71; 93–95.

19. William Frankena, *Ethics* (Englewood Cliffs, New Jersey: Prentice-Hall, Inc., 1973), p. 53.

20. MacIntyre, *After Virtue*, 178.

Chapter 2

Ethics, Epistemology,
and the Expert

Until very recently, scientists made rigid distinctions between facts and objectivity on the one hand and values and subjectivity on the other hand. Committed as they were to the search for truth, natural and social scientists were attracted to the teachings of positivism, which are usually summarized as follows:

1. All knowledge is found in sense experience.
2. Meaning is grounded in observations.
3. Concepts and generalizations only *represent* the particulars from which they have been abstracted; they do not exist in themselves.
4. The sciences are unified according to the methodology of the natural sciences. The ideal pursued in knowledge is the form of a mathematically formulated universal science deducible from the smallest possible number of axioms.
5. Values are not facts, and hence values cannot be given as such in sense experience. Since all knowledge is based on sense experience, value judgments cannot be accorded the status of knowledge claims.[1]

Eager to make progress toward truth and away from falsity, scientists and technicians adhered to these five tenets, eschewing values as merely subjective choices, decisions, preferences, or commitments, and embracing facts as objective manifestations of reality. Their efforts to attain certain knowledge were carefully monitored by policymakers who hoped that science and technology could help them render government rational and efficient. Thus, policymakers dismissed scientists and technicians, who were unable to separate value judgments from factual statements, as little better than myth makers, storytellers, or witch doctors. Why hire a policy expert for analysis and advice, asked the government official, if he or she is just as benighted, befuddled, and bewildered as one's cronies? In contrast, policymakers heralded as a veritable savior any scientist or technician who could separate the

Siamese twins of fact and value. At last, exclaimed the government official, we have found someone who can give us an objective estimate about what *is*, rather than what merely *seems* to be, the best course for the ship of state, and this person is the policy expert—a man or woman trained in one of the natural, social, or mathematical sciences who aggressively defends neutral facts from the assault of biased values.

Admittedly, there is something seductive about neutral facts, for they promise us security—an infallible guide in our struggle for survival. The fact that positivism promised us truth, rationality, objectivity, and certitude—the facts and nothing but the facts—explains why it held sway for so long. But if we have learned anything, it is that the facts are not always enough. During World War II, for example, the separation of politics and ethics from science led scientists to provide key technical aid to projects which, from a moral standpoint, were problematic at best. One instance of this is the case of Wernher von Braun, who worked on the Nazi atom bomb and rocketry program, and then, after the war, began working for the U.S. government's rocketry program. Fairly or unfairly, von Braun has been caricatured even by pop singers as an "amoral technician" interested only in the mechanics of his tasks.[2]

Von Braun's image highlights the problems that haunt the relationship between policy experts and policymakers. When the knowledgeable speak to the powerful, there is always the risk that knowledge will become merely the servant of power, with no say in the way that it is used. The positivist legacy merely helped institutionalize this dangerous separation of fact (provided by those with knowledge) from value (decided on by those with power), making policy experts content to leave the political and ethical problems up to those who solicited their analysis and advice. The saga of Robert Oppenheimer and his colleagues illustrates this only too well. According to Freeman Dyson, author of *Disturbing the Universe*, most scientists working on the Los Alamos project gave little thought to the political and ethical ramifications of their work. Instead, they gloried in the pleasure of working with some of the most brilliant scientific minds of the day toward the joint solution of fascinating technical problems. Only after the atom bomb was exploded at Hiroshima and Nagasaki, and after the spectre of an uncontrolled arms race began looming, did some scientists directly confront the full implications of their invention. In 1948 Oppenheimer stated, "In some sort of crude sense, which no vulgarity, no humor, no overstatement can quite extinguish, the physicists have known sin; and this is a knowledge which they cannot lose."[3] No longer willing or even able to hide from themselves the moral dimensions of their work, many physicists—Oppenheimer among them—then threw themselves into the political arena, trying both to educate the public regarding the prodigious new forces that had been unleashed and to assure them that these forces would be harnessed in a humane way.

Increasingly aware of the ways in which values permeate their work, contemporary policy experts are questioning not only the consequences of value-free science, but its very possibility. Since these critiques are too many and varied to cover exhaustively, I will limit myself to those that have been leveled against such techniques of expertise as cost-benefit analysis and risk-benefit analysis. Although I am convinced that there are problems with value-laden as well as value-free policy analysis—they can both be misused and abused—I nevertheless believe that it is better for us to admit rather than to deny the ways in which values and facts fuse together. Provided that policy experts are able and willing to identify and articulate the ways in which their epistemologies, ethics, and politics intersect, and provided they admit to themselves as well as to us that their work is qualitative, relative, value-laden, culturally defined, and subjectively conceptualized, their contributions to the policy process should be welcomed for what they are: the soundest base for forging a policy that serves the public's best interests.

ANALYTIC TECHNIQUES: A CRITIQUE
OF COST-BENEFIT
AND RISK-BENEFIT ANALYSIS

Cost-Benefit Analysis

Originally used in the sphere of natural resources management, cost-benefit analysis is now the preferred mode of analysis in all departments of the government bureaucracy. Although economists and other policy experts had been supplying the government with facts and figures routinely since the New Deal, the high inflation rates of the 1970s prompted then President Ford to issue Executive Order 11821, which required all federal agencies to quantify and publish the costs and benefits of anticipated new standards in the form of "Inflationary Impact Statements." The Office of Management and Budget (OMB) put this order into effect, requiring that cost-benefit studies be conducted if a newly proposed standard would affect any of six areas: cost, productivity, energy supply and demand, critical materials, employment, or market structure. Thus, if the Environmental Protection Agency (EPA) wanted to protect workers from toxic death by regulating arsenic emissions from copper-smelter plants, it had to specify in advance the costs as well as the benefits of its proposed regulation. If the costs of life-preserving controls were estimated to be so high as to deprive not only the industrialists of their profits but also the workers of their jobs and the nation of adequate copper supplies, then the EPA would be required to withdraw its proposal in favor of one less solicitous. Despite some murmuring about the ethical implications of making such trade-offs, President Carter reissued Ford's executive order mandating cost-benefit analysis, as did Carter's successor, Ronald Reagan.[4]

The process of cost-benefit analysis has several major steps, including the definition of desired goals, the determination of alternative means for accomplishing the desired goals, the determination of the costs and benefits of each of the alternative means, the comparison and ranking of each alternative's costs and benefits, and adjustments in terms of "major uncertainties" that may have skewed the analysis.[5] Although this quantitative process is supposed to provide policymakers with a rational and impartial basis upon which to forge public policy, we may sometimes suspect that no matter what our friendly policymakers in Washington, D.C. say, cost-benefit analysis is just as irrational and ideological as pork-barreling or logrolling. Certainly, cost-benefit analysis is not as value-free as it was originally held out to be.

A Sociologist's Critique of Cost-Benefit Analysis. In recent years, the public's suspicions have been expressed in sociological form by Ida R. Hoos. Dr. Hoos criticizes cost-benefit analysis for two reasons: (1) it encourages "piecemeal fragmentation," a tunnel-visioned concentration on the measurable parts of a policy problem rather than on the whole; and (2) it elicits a drive toward "scientific objectivity" which "turns out to be neither scientific nor objective."[6] As a prime example of a cost-benefit analysis that represents "piecemeal fragmentation" at its worst, Hoos refers to a 1967 California State Department of Public Health study of solid waste management. In their attempt to identify the optimal solid waste system for not only the Fresno region but the entire nation, cost-benefit analysts asked thirty-nine people to rank, in order of odiousness, thirteen bad effects of a poor waste-management system (e.g., flies, air or water pollution, rodents, human or animal disease, odor). From this molehill, the analysts generated a mountain of data—to be specific, 25,000 bits![7]

Finding nothing pretentious about their claims, the analysts proclaimed that "*any* waste management's performance effectiveness can be gauged by the degree of reduction of these . . . bad effects." (italics mine)."[8] In response to this outbreak of hubris, Hoos suggests that by focusing on their 25,000 bits of data, the cost-benefit analysts failed to thematize the very large social, cultural, and philosophical question implicit in any serious study of waste: Namely, do we as individuals and as a nation waste too much? If so, one way to solve the waste-management problem is not by spending millions of dollars on pest control, but simply by each one of us wasting less.

Not content to confine herself to cost-benefit analyses that fail to see the forest for the trees, Hoos goes on to challenge analyses that produce neither "objective" nor "scientific" cost-benefit estimates. Typical of these biased estimates is, in her opinion, the supersonic transport cost-benefit study. The way Hoos understands it, government policy analysts deliberately underestimated not only the dollar cost of the SST but also its social costs. For example, Hoos notes that the analysts asked *engineers*—and not physicians, psychologists, or psychiatrists, as might be expected—to test young, healthy, and prepared adults for sonic boom stress. Infants, the aged, the nervous, and the unprepared—precisely the persons most susceptible to sonic boom stress—were not included in the study. Similarly, while the analysts gladly quoted studies that pooh-poohed environmental degradation, they squelched studies that projected a deleterious depletion of the stratospheric ozone layer without which the earth is defenseless against solar ultraviolet radiation. Observes Hoos:

> With dollar costs minimized, opportunity costs omitted, and social costs ignored, the balance with respect to benefits was made to appear so overwhelming that opponents were regarded as latter-day Luddites, pitiable in their feeble attempt to stay the mighty advance of the state-of-the-art, or

benighted traitors, advocating that their country voluntarily surrender its enviable position of technical leadership in the air transport world.[9]

In the end—but only after seven years of deliberation, a $700 million expenditure, and some very misleading analysis and advice—the U.S. Senate began to add up the costs of the SST system for itself and voted 51 to 46 to discontinue federal appropriations for it. What disturbs Hoos most about this episode, other than the deceptions that apparently characterized it, is precisely the fact that it took policymakers so long to wake up. Hoos wonders how often policymakers are either unwilling or unable to reject dubious scientific analysis and advice for fear of being exposed as ignoramuses.

A Philosopher's Critique of Cost-Benefit Analysis. Hoos's sociological concerns are given normative backing by many philosophers including Alasdair MacIntyre. He argues that utilitarians and cost-benefit analysts flock together because they are birds of the same moral feather. Supposedly, utilitarians are able to add and subtract hedons (units of pleasure) and dolors (units of pain) without any signs of cognitive or affective distress simply because they have decided in advance that human experience ought to be structured and evaluated in terms of pleasure and pain, and that we ought to perform that action which, more than any alternative action, produces a greater balance of pleasure over pain. The world the utilitarian inhabits "is one in which questions of value have become questions of fact and in which the aim and the vindication of theory is its success in increasing our manipulative powers."[10] So, too, the world the cost-benefit analyst inhabits is, by MacIntyre's account, one in which questions of value (What is the worth of one human life?) become questions of fact (How many dollars does it cost to keep Grandpa Jones on a respirator?). Far from being a neutral methodology, attuned to neutral facts, MacIntyre describes cost-benefit analysis as contemporary bureaucracy's most important device "for ensuring that thought, perception and action are organized in a utilitarian way."[11]

In his widely anthologized critique, "Utilitarianism and Cost/Benefit Analysis: An Essay on the Relevance of Moral Philosophy to Bureaucratic Theory," MacIntyre goes on to discuss at length what he perceives to be the five major deficiencies of cost-benefit analysis. First, dominated as it is by the almighty dollar, cost-benefit analysis fails to consider the relative costs and benefits of an indeterminately large range of alternatives, choosing to focus single-mindedly on a highly restricted set of currently profitable alternatives. Cost-benefit analysts cater to current consumer preferences. They give the consumers what they want at an affordable price. By simply assuming that consumer markets are given rather than made, cost-benefit analysts contribute to the ossification of society's current values. Second, the use of cost-benefit analysis presupposes not only a prior decision as to what counts as a cost and as a benefit, but also a prior selection of a scale for ranking otherwise incommensurable costs and benefits. For example, a cost-benefit analyst may either explicitly or implicitly subscribe to a hierarchy of values according to which quantity of life ranks higher than quality of life. If so, this analyst will probably produce a study that weighs increased life span due to clean air and water more heavily than decreased job security due to an industry's inability to pay for mandated air and water pollution controls. Another analyst who values quality of life over quantity of life will probably produce a study that emphasizes the costs of decreased job security and minimizes the benefits of increased life span. Third, the application of cost-benefit analysis presupposes a decision as to **whose** values—the policy experts', the policymakers', the affected parties', the general public's—are to count in the weighing of costs and benefits. Fourth, cost-benefit analysis has no way of deter-mining how far into the future the consequences of a particular policy should be considered. Fifth and finally, the advocates of cost-benefit analysis cannot deal adequately with unpredictability due to shifts in human needs, wants, and desires as well as to technological innovations, environmental changes, population fluctua-tions, and so on.[12]

Sociological and Philosophical Defenses of Cost-Benefit Analysis. Although MacIntyre's critique is powerful when directed against either textbook portrayals or popular versions of cost-benefit analysis, philosopher Tom L. Beauchamp and policy analyst Vincent Vacarro both argue that it is relatively forceless when directed against the actual practice of cost-benefit analysis within the government bureau-cracy. Admittedly, textbook portrayals of cost-benefit analysis do speak as if all the elements of a problem are calculable and predictable. And, as MacIntyre suggests, such a presentation of cost-benefit analysis may put policymakers and policy experts under pressure both to treat the inestimable as calculable, (or the unpre-dictable as knowable) and to ignore any arbitrariness involved in so doing. But, claims Beauchamp and especially Vacarro, once most policy analysts get out of graduate school—indeed, even before they leave their ivory towers—they realize that the unpredictable and inestimable can no more be ignored than the way in which their values affect the facts they report. Indeed, most good practitioners of policy analysis are well aware that they are making judgment calls, that they are engaged in an exercise of practical reasoning.[13]

Defense I. Eager to defend cost-benefit analysis, Beauchamp, Vacarro, and others offer a point-by-point rebuttal of MacIntyre's five charges. In response to the charge that cost-benefit analysts think only in economic terms, they argue first that although cost-benefit analysis does focus on economic factors, it in no way ignores noneconomic considerations, including references both to the production of new values and to the maintenance of already treasured values. Vacarro insists that cost-benefit analysts are routinely encouraged to flag noneconomic considerations for two reasons: (1) a policy of flagging values alongside an analysis is to be preferred to a policy of embedding values in an analysis where a policymaker is likely to mis-take them for "facts"; and (2) what makes cost-benefit analysis a valuable tool for policymakers is precisely its ability to identify and clarify nonquantifiable as well as quantifiable costs and benefits.[14] Vacarro writes as if policymakers eagerly turn to the margins and footnotes of their experts' analyses, expecting to find there the really important policy recommendations. Other policy analysts, Burton A. Weisbrod among them, however, indicate that the situation is otherwise.

> Whatever cannot be expressed in terms of the common-denominator metric at the heart of the analysis is either *excluded* from consideration, simply noted outside of the analysis itself from the decision-maker's *possible use*, or at *most incorporated into the analysis in the form of a constraint*—a qualitative requirement, subject to which the project is designed so as to maximize benefits minus costs. (italics mine)[15]

Clearly, Weisbrod's choice of words suggests that qualitative considerations are regarded by policymakers and experts alike as some sort of cloying frosting that detracts from the taste of an elegant numerical cake, or as some sort of disagreeable medicine (constraint) that paradoxically prevents experts from identifying the most beneficial and least costly cure for a salient social woe and policymakers from administering it. Thus, if Weisbrod's (and not Vacarro's) reading of "flagging" is correct, then MacIntyre's first critique of cost-benefit analysis remains undefeated: Cost-benefit analysis has everything to do with *quantifiable* costs and benefits, and very little, if anything, to do with elusive concerns of quality.

Defense II. Defenders of cost-benefit analysis answer MacIntyre's second charge by admitting that they are indeed trying to render otherwise incommensurable items commensurable, but that there is nothing inherently illogical or immoral about this attempt provided that adequate methods or techniques for ranking can be formulated. Significantly, MacIntyre admits that if such standards could be formulated, cost-benefit analysis would have us on our way to the Promised Land. What MacIntyre argues, however, is that depending on whether she is from the Brookings Institute or whether he is from the Hoover Institute, the cost-benefit analyst will come up with radically different ranking methods or techniques. For example, MacIntyre notes that cost-benefit analysts have at least four alternative methods for computing the cost of a person's life: (1) discounting to the present the person's expected future earnings; (2) first identifying the expected future losses to significant others from the person's death and then discounting them to the present; (3) determining the value placed on human life by current social policies and practices (e.g., the fact that most of us are presently prepared to accept the tragic costs of a high fatal accident rate in order to enjoy the benefits of relatively unrestricted, voluminous motor traffic says something about how much we do or do not value human life per se); and (4) directly ascertaining what value a person places on his or her own life, by determining which risks that person is or was prepared to take and which insurance costs he or she is or was ready to pay.[16] MacIntyre notes that, depending on which of these methods the analyst selects, he or she will produce quite different recommendations, and that because such a choice of methods is "arbitrary," the analysis is somehow suspect.

Significantly, many defenders of cost-benefit analysis frankly admit that value preferences do indeed influence analysts' choice of methodology and therefore the way in which they present the facts. However, this influence is not pernicious provided that the analyst is aware of it, presents and defends it as a theoretical choice, and documents alternative assumptions for policymakers' consideration. Only analysts who are value-oriented are able to identify and articulate the ways in which ethical, political, and social concerns interpret their methodologies. Only they are likely, for example, first to see what is morally unacceptable about a certain methodology and then to explain in what the unacceptability consists to concerned policymakers and citizens.

In all fairness to the advocates of cost-benefit analysis, it should be pointed out that MacIntyre simply laments the fact that analysts can arbitrarily pick from at least four life-valuing methodologies without going on to consider the ways in which these methodologies have been challenged on moral grounds from within as well as from without the policy analysis community. In recent years the discounted-future-earnings approach (DFE), for example, has drawn particularly heavy fire. DFE takes the average age at which death of people killed by a given type of accident or disease occurs and computes what their expected future income would have been if they had lived a normal life span. It then discounts this expected future income, since a dollar received today can be invested and thus worth more than a dollar received tomorrow (especially in periods of rampant inflation). The resulting figure is termed the "present value" of life for the average member of the group in question. Because young adult white males still have, on the average, better expected future earning power than any other societal group, DFE figures can and do yield discriminatory policy recommendations. Steven E. Rhoads, for example, reports that in the mid-1960s

> ... studies suggested that a media campaign encouraging the wearing of motorcycle helmets might save a life for $3,000. A cervix cancer program could do almost as well—$3,250 per life saved. Yet DFE figures prevented the programs from being close competitors. The benefit-cost ratio for the motorcycle program was 55.6, while for the cervix cancer program it was only 8.9[17]

In sum, because women's lifes are not currently as "valuable" as men's lives, they are not currently worth as much money.

Because of DFE's biased structure, a structure that tends to reinforce patterns of discrimination, some cost-benefit analysts were won over to the willingness-to-pay approach (WTP), not because WTP is necessarily more efficient than DFE but because it is inherently more equitable. Supposedly, the willingness-to-pay approach is more equitable because the value it puts on human life is determined not by a person's discounted future earnings—which are, in many respects, beyond a person's control—but by a person's willingness to pay to avoid possible death.[18] Unfortunately, it is notoriously difficult to determine, for example, how much Joe is willing to pay for a medical program or an antipollution campaign that will increase his chances of living an extra two, five, ten, or fifteen years. Some cost-benefit analysts favor polls as a measure of willingness-to-pay. Others look to decisions that individuals make when their lives are actually at risk. Both methods are riddled with difficulties, however. Respondents to polls may engage in strategic behavior, understating or overstating their real WTP in order to shift the average WTP and resulting cost burdens in ways that benefit them, or they may fail to understand and give consistent answers to the questions posed.[19] Similarly, those whose lives are at actual risk—a high-rise construction worker, for example—may say that yes, in theory, his chosen occupation is more risky than most, but because of his superior scaffold-crawling skills it isn't really that risky *for him* in practice.

As difficult as these distortions are to handle, the most serious difficulty that plagues the WTP approach is the fact that a cost-benefit analysis makes ethical sense only "if the notions of benefits and costs are connected in a certain way with the notions of human well-being or welfare or happiness."[20] But since people frequently prefer states of affairs which do not increase their well-being, welfare, or happiness, not only the WTP methodology in particular but cost-benefit analysis, predicated as it is on utilitarian values, may be ethically incoherent. This, I take it, is what philosophers like K. S. Shrader-Frechette have against cost-benefit analysis as it is sometimes practiced. Hearkening back to MacIntyre's first criticism of cost-benefit analysis, Shrader-Frechette observes that cost benefit analysts usually fail to distinguish between the satisfaction of wants and the achievement of authentic well being. To illustrate her point, Shrader-Frechette refers to a recent OTA assessment of private automobile use. Since the authors of the study pointed out every fashion of cost associated with automobile use—high oil and gasoline prices, high insurance premiums, highway congestion and accompanying tension headaches, risk of serious accident, creation of hazardous levels of air pollution—it came as a surprise when they nonetheless concluded that these costs did not outweigh the benefit(s) Americans get from clinging to their primary symbol and means of mobility. Largely because most Americans *prefer* their personal automobiles to public transportation, the OTA assessors concluded that no cost—short of certain death, I suppose—could outweigh Americans' supposed "unalienable right" to drive their very own dream machines. What disturbs Shrader-Frechette about this analysis is that consumer preferences are taken as the "criterion for the value placed on certain costs and benefits" without any effort to assess the comparative worth of these preferences.[21] No matter how trivial, how stupid, or how evil, a preference is a preference is a preference.

Of course, there are ways both to meet Shrader-Frechette's general objection to an over-reliance on consumer preference and to handle particular cases like the person who prefers to spend his extra money on much-wanted watermelon jelly beans rather than on much-needed health insurance, and that is by exemplifying the much-beloved ideal of "rational preference."—What an individual would pay for much-needed health insurance under certain ideal conditions (after he carefully reflects on the difference between a crying need and a whimsical want, takes into account all the relevant information about his circumstances, and takes great care to use all his reasoning power to the best of his ability).[22] Not unexpectedly, the major problem with rational preferences is that they are just as difficult to ascertain as "irrational" or "nonrational" preferences. Very few of us can say what, under ideal circumstances of knowledge, would be a rational amount to pay to save our lives and limbs from risk. Is a third-rate pianist, who loves playing the piano more perhaps than life itself, operating within the limits of reason when she insures her fingers for $1,000,000? Is 60 year-old Grandpa Jones acting rationally when he refuses to spend the money he has squirreled away for his grand-children's college education on his much-needed kidney dialysis treatment? I, for one, do not have pat answers to these questions, and even if I did, I suspect that the WTP approach would remain vulnerable to a more serious challenge; namely, its tendency to reinforce class lines. Whereas a rich woman may be willing to pay $100 or even $1000 to make her car slightly safer, a poor woman may consider such an expenditure a waste of money. This is not because the poor woman values her "poor" life less than the rich woman values her "rich" life, or even because the poor woman is less rational than the rich woman. Rather, it is simply a reflec-tion of the disparities that exist between the poor and the rich woman. The rich woman knows full well that if she spends an extra $100 or $1000 for a safer auto-mobile, she will still have money for her daughter's ballet lessons, her husband's birthday present, and her new cruise clothes. In contrast, the poor woman knows full well that if she spends an extra $100 or even an extra $10 on a safer auto-mobile, she will have substantially reduced or even exhausted her meager dis-cretionary funds, funds that she may have been squirreling away for her own long-deferred college education.

Given that the idea of "rational preference" is largely unworkable, there are, says Steven Rhoads, only two obvious ways to equalize the amount of money people are willing to spend on life-extending means. We can either place direct restrictions on rich persons' health expenditures or tax the rich in order to sub-sidize the poor's health. But if we believe that it is wrong to restrict the freedom of the rich either by forbidding them to spend as much as they desire on prolong-ing their own lives or by taxing them, against their own wills, in order to guarantee every poor person the longest life possible, then we must abandon the WTP approach. According to Ezra Mishan, however, there are ways to amend the WTP approach, thereby rendering it less morally suspect. When we are asked to deter-mine, for example, whether people are willing to pay for a sickle-cell anemia screening program for poor Blacks, then we may add the willingness of any rich person to pay for this program to the willingness of any poor person to pay for it. The problem with this amendation is that its WTP quotient is based on the advan-taged person's subjective sense of satisfaction; he or she just happens to derive psychic pleasure from the thought of alleviating the disadvantaged person's suffer-ing. But once we factor into our analysis the **subjective satisfactions** of those who might feel better as more lives are saved, then, logically, we must also incorporate the **subjective dissatisfactions** of those who might feel worse as these added lives are saved.[23] Steven Rhoads opines that on Mishan's account:

> ... an analysis of a health program especially effective in reducing the risk of death for the elderly would add the WTP of the elderly, their friends, family, and the public at large—but then subtract from this total the amount necessary to compensate any greedy heirs for the decrease in their welfare

resulting from the possible lengthening of the lives of their eventual bene-
factors.[24]

Still, Mishan's analysis could be further amended to avoid such abhorrent results by
factoring into the WTP of the rich not their *subjective sense of satisfaction* at the
sight and sound of longer-lived poor people, but their *objective sense of duty* to
human persons less fortunate than themselves. Arguably, no rich person—if he or
she is at all rational—is without this sense of duty. I take it that this is what Kant
means when he argues that the maxim, "Let each one be as happy as heaven wills,
or as he can make himself; I will not take anything from him or even envy him;
but to his welfare or to his assistance in time of need I have no desire to contribute," would not be universalized as a law of nature by rational persons because
instances can arise in which they "would need the love and sympathy of others,"
and in which they would have "robbed" themselves, by virtue of the law
they had universalized, of all "hope" of desired aid.[25] Of course, cost-benefit
analysts are not accustomed to factoring duties into their computations. And,
assuredly, Kant may be wrong; were the shoes of fortune reversed, there may be
those among us who would not desire the love and sympathy of others. But, on the
face of it, it seems no more difficult to measure an objective sense of duty than a
subjective sense of satisfaction; and I really doubt that very many rational persons
are prepared to starve to death rather than to admit the fundamental ties of decency
that bind human beings together. Although the WTP approach, like the DFE
approach, is ethically flawed as it stands, there may be ways to remedy its most
egregious deviations from those norms of human welfare we most treasure. If not,
the WTP approach should be drowned in the same alphabet soup that drowned the
DFE approach, thereby adding stock to MacIntyre's claim that cost-benefit analysis
is not only embarassingly subjective but morally pernicious.

Defense III. MacIntyre's third objection to cost-benefit analysis—that it fails to
consider in great enough detail the question of who in society should bear the costs
of a project and who should reap the benefits—is more difficult for defenders of
cost-benefit analysis to meet. Vincent Vacarro observes that cost-benefit analysts
have been able and willing to accommodate questions of allocative efficiency but
not of distributional equity.[26] So-called "allocative benefits" refer to those effects
of a project that are characterized either by increases in consumer satisfaction or
by decreases in the cost of resources required to produce goods and services. For
example, an improvement in the water quality of a lake may be reflected by the
amount local residents are willing to pay for the additional enjoyment of swimming.
So-called "distributional benefits" refer to changes in some people's well-being at
the expense of the well-being of others. For example, improvement in the water
quality of the lake and an accompanying increase in swimming might raise the
price of swimwear. As a result, the sellers of swimwear would experience a dollar
gain and the buyers of the latest aquatic fashions would experience a dollar loss.
Thus, what this situation represents is an income transfer from the buyers to the
sellers of swimwear.

In general, cost-benefit analysts have argued that it is not their job to judge distributional issues like the dollar gains of one group versus the dollar losses of another group. So, for example, a team of OTA cost-benefit analysts recently concluded that slurry pipelines can transport coal more economically than any other mode of transport. Simply assuming that it is legal to ignore questions of equity in distribution, the analysts ignored the fact that whereas Far Westerners would be "negatively affected by slurry use of scarce water resources," Midwesterners and Easterners would be "positively affected by receiving Western coal."[27] This non-judgemental stance not always withstanding, some thoughtful analysts are attempting to accommodate questions of distribution by introducing a theory of compensation into their calculations. Admittedly, these efforts are still rudimentary, primarily because most theories of compensation are phrased in hypothetical terms, requiring only that losers could be compensated in some perfect (but nonexistent) system of transfers. Critics complain that "unless those harmed by a decision are *actually* compensated, they will get little solace from the fact that someone is reaping a surplus in which they could have shared."[28] Still people may have more good will than the critics admit—perhaps harmdoers will do more than they are required to do and voluntarily compensate the harmed.[29] Nevertheless, those of us who are cynical—who trust in the rule of law rather than in the innate generosity of men and women—may have more confidence in a theory of compensation that requires losers to be actually compensated "or else." Such a theory, however, has yet to be conceived. Moreover, as K. S. Shrader-Frechette points out, compensation is not necessarily a panacea. Suppose, she says, that one set of persons is made better off by a total of $10x$ dollars at the expense of another set of individuals who are made worse off by $1x$ dollars. Since the group as a whole is $9x$ dollars better off today than yesterday, and since the group that suffered will, *ex hypothesi*, be compensated by at least $1x$ dollars for its losses, what can Shrader-Frechette's complaint be? It is, if I am not mistaken, that although the poor are not getting poorer, the rich are getting richer, thereby increasing the gap between these two classes and thus the relative poverty of the poor.

Defenses IV and V. In contrast to MacIntyre's third criticism of cost-benefit analysis, his fourth and fifth objections to it are initially easily countered. MacIntyre notwithstanding, many cost-benefit analysts insist that they do take long-range, indirect consequences (externalities) into account, and they are well aware that uncertainty is the name of the game. According to E. S. Quade, the ideal cost-benefit analysis takes all costs and benefits into account, including those that span the life of the project. It incorporates the individual consequences of any project—the so-called externalities, side effects, and spillovers—such as the roadside business that is ruined because the new lake diverts traffic or the beach that increased shipping renders unsuitable for swimming. The ideal cost-benefit analysis also incorporates uncertainty about any economic, technical, and operational parameters that can be quantified: listed, measured, or estimated.[31]

Despite Quade's optimism, some of his colleagues observe that even when externalities are taken into account, they often have a way of being discounted. For example, an OTA study of the direct use of coal took into consideration not only the relevant economic and technological costs and benefits, but also the salient social and even aesthetic impacts. After weighing all the pros and cons, the study drew a conclusion favorable to the direct use of coal on the grounds that its clear and certain economic benefits far outweighed such murky and uncertain externalities as "nonmarket factors associated with coal use."[32] The market, it seems, is a sure bet—a perfectly predictable beast!

Conclusion. Despite the criticisms that we have just directed against cost-benefit analysis, it probably does not have all the flaws Alasdair MacIntyre attributes to utilitarianism. For one thing, there are junctures at which nonutilitarian values can enter into a cost-benefit analysis. For another, it is clear that cost-benefit analysts are increasingly willing and able to make use of these access points. Nevertheless, there are times when cost-benefit analysis seems a morally inappropriate technique to use precisely because it cannot accommodate the values we want it to accommodate. For example, in 1978, acting under the authority of the Occupational Safety and Health Act, the then Secretary of Labor issued a rule designed to limit workers' exposure to cotton dust, invoking "the most protective standard possible." The cotton industry protested the standard, insisting that the act required that before a protective standard could be invoked it had first to be justified by a cost-benefit analysis. After much deliberation, the Supreme Court ruled in favor of the workers, declaring that the intention of the act was "to place preeminent value on assuring employees a safe and healthful working environment."[33] As a result of the Supreme Court's ruling, OSHA was precluded from complying with an executive order requiring cost-benefit analyses of all federal regulations. It was not precluded, however, from using cost-effectiveness analyses, which would allow it to set standards that reach health and safety goals in the least expensive way possible. For example, although it is an uncontestable goal of OSHA that workers be protected from toxic pollutants in the work place, industries may achieve this goal in the least expensive way possible, be it by built-in engineering controls to remove the hazard, personal protective gear such as respirators to insulate workers from the hazard, medical monitoring to assure that the hazard is not affecting the health of workers, or some combination of these.[34]

On the surface, such a compromise seems eminently reasonable. Workers' rights are not sacrificed to industries' utilities, but the industries are not totally deprived of their utilities. In the same way that one can fly to Paris either first or second class, supposedly a worker's lungs can be protected by more or less expensive means. According to some critics, however, industries are likely to strap their workers to seats on top of that plane headed for Paris; that is, they and their analysts are likely to insist that a given means of protection is adequate, when in point of fact it is very inadequate. In sum, like cost-benefit analysis, cost-effectiveness analysis is always vulnerable to recalcitrant analysts who refuse to submit to the discipline of those values without which we cannot hope to remain human.

Risk-Benefit Analysis

Largely because it takes into account possible and probable costs as well as actual costs, risk-benefit analysis is regarded as a qualitative improvement over cost-benefit analysis and its variants. The threefold task of the risk-benefit analyst is to estimate how likely it is that some harmful event will occur, how many people will be affected by it, and to what degree, and what measures can and should be taken to avert or to minimize it. At bottom, risk-benefit analysis is an estimate of the extent to which the public is or is not willing to tolerate a particular risk. Although the risk of injury, illness, or death has always been with humankind, the last few decades have shown rapid increases in both the levels of risk to which we are exposed and in our consciousness of them. This growing preoccupation with risk is largely the product of "technological disillusionment," the realization that technology is not an unalloyed blessing, but one that poses risks to life and limb.[35]

Problems with Risk Assessment. As we become more cognizant of risk, the method by which risks are assessed increases in importance. Risk assessment is a two-step process that includes both an *estimate of risk* (a determination of the magnitude of an adverse effect and the probability that it will occur) and a *decision of acceptability* with reference to the estimated risk. Both steps of the process are shot through with epistemological problems. For example, most estimates of risk consist in pitting "objective measures" of risk against "subjective measures" of risk. Objective measures of risk describe the real or actual risk of a policy. Using either mathematical calculations or experimental evidence, "objectivists" estimate the statistical probability of a dam bursting or the likelihood of saccharin causing cancer. In contrast to objective measures, subjective measures describe the perceptions of those assessing the risk. As might be anticipated, objective and subjective measurements of risk often fail to agree.[36] For example, although the risk-benefit analysts who wrote the Rasmussen Report ("Reactor Safety Study: An Assessment of Accident Risks in U.S. Commercial Nuclear Power Plants") concluded that fission reactors present only a minimal threat to the public,[37] citizens—especially those who lived near nuclear power plants—perceived themselves at considerable risk.

When objective and subjective determinations of risk differ, two extreme solutions seem immediately evident. One approach is to insist on using only objective measures of risk in policymaking and to ignore public perceptions. This solution is generally met with public dissatisfaction. But to the extent that policymakers are able and willing to ignore public protest, this approach facilitates, in the opinion of many experts, what is ultimately the most effective protection against risk. After all, if parents ought not to cater excessively to their children's irrational fears of imaginary gremlins, goblins, and ghosts, then policymakers ought not to cater to their constituencies' ungrounded suspicions, phobias, and paranoias. Directly opposed to this paternalistic approach is one that focuses only on public perceptions of risk, giving priority to those programs that will minimize the perceived risk. Such an approach, while designed to still short-term public fear, can often result in a misdirection of priorities away from programs that would provide the greatest possible protection from actual risk in the long run.

Paradoxically, objective measurements of risk are not necessarily more accurate than subjective measurements of risk. In the case of the much-touted Rasmussen Report, the scientists' objective measurement of risk ("Don't worry folks, everything is under control") turned out to be less accurate than many citizens' subjective assessments ("One of those nuclear reactors is bound to malfunction sooner or later—and probably sooner"). According to K. S. Shrader-Frechette, four serious methodological problems discredited the Rasmussen Report's fundamental assumption, namely that the probability of a catastrophic nuclear accident is so minuscule as to be unimportant. First, the Rasmussen Report relied upon a now-discredited mathematical model termed "fault tree analysis," which provides no way to account for all the causal factors that can contribute to an accident. For example, Rasmussen *et al*. performed their calculations worrying neither about the aging and deterioration of the plant nor about the possibility of terrorist attacks and sabotage. Second, the Rasmussen Report seriously underestimated the number of cancers and genetic damages that would be triggered by a serious nuclear accident. Whereas the Rasmussen team predicted 310 fatal cancers, the prestigious American Physical Society predicted somewhere between 10,000 and 15,000.[38] Third, the Rasmussen Report based its sanguine prophecies about the reliability of the emergency core cooling systems of nuclear reactors not on long experience or on experimental evidence, but on flawed computerized calculations and on small scale-model tests, all of which failed to demonstrate the supposed safety of the cooling systems.[39] Fourth, the authors of the report blithely assumed that 90-percent evacuation could be accomplished around any imperiled nuclear power plant, including those located in heavily populated areas, even though warning time would be extremely short and despite the fact that no evacuation plans had ever been evaluated or empirically tested.[40]

Problems with Risk Acceptability. Assuming that risk-benefit analysts can overcome the methodological handicaps that impede their ability to estimate risk accurately, they would have to refine their techniques further in order to ascertain not only *how much* of a danger a hazard really poses, but *how acceptable* this hazard is when its risks are weighed against its benefits. Shrader-Frechette notes that if the Rasmussen Report and similar studies reflect the state of the art, then risk-benefit analysts have to provide more convincing studies before she, for one, accepts the risks of having a nuclear power plant near her house. In particular, Shrader-Frechette is singularly unimpressed by the three major arguments that have been forwarded on behalf of the friendly neighborhood nuclear reactor:

1.   That, since the core-melt probability is approximately 5×10^{-5} per reactor per year, the public has only a small risk from a possible nuclear accident;

2.   That, since society accepts other risks whose consequences are more disastrous than those of nuclear power, the risk of a major nuclear accident also ought to be accepted; and

3. That, although a nuclear accident would cause 5000 cancer deaths, 3000 cases of genetic damage, and numerous instances of thyroid disease, since "the small increases in these diseases would not be detected" and would be "insignificant compared to those eight million injuries caused annually by other accidents," the risk of a nuclear accident ought to be accepted.[41]

As Shrader-Frechette sees it, since all three of these arguments fail, the friendly neighborhood nuclear reactor is not necessarily a more acceptable risk than the friendly shark in the local lagoon.

Argument 1 Countered. With respect to the first argument on the above list, Shrader-Frechette argues that even if the probability of a meltdown is 1 in 17,000—a dubious estimate—it is not clear that low probability of catastrophe is a sufficient condition for acceptable risk. Just because a risk has a very low probability of resulting in catastrophe and a very high probability of producing economic benefits does not mean that the risk ought to be accepted. The defenders of nuclear risk simply assume that the reigning economic order is good, and that any means necessary for maintaining this good (inexpensive nuclear energy) is also good. Never do they challenge the "goodness" of the status quo, a state of affairs that requires the United States to use, misuse, and waste two to three times the per capita energy of other Western developed nations.[42]

Argument 2 Countered. With respect to the second argument, Shrader-Frechette observes that just because risk x is lower than morally acceptable risk y does not mean that risk x is just as or even more morally acceptable than risk y. Perhaps risk x, unlike risk y, has been imposed on those who must live with it—or die on account of it—without either their knowledge or their consent. Thus, to the degree that we believe that only voluntary risks ought to be accepted on moral grounds, to that same degree will we tend to find risk x—however low—morally unacceptable. What makes a risk voluntary is that we assume it in knowledge and with power. We assume it, that is, informed of all relevant facts and known contingencies, and free of all external coercion or internal compulsion. According to Joel Feinberg, among the factors that tend to defeat ascriptions of full responsibility are neurotic compulsion, misinformation, excitement or impetuousness, clouded judgment as from alcohol or drugs, or immature or defective faculties of reasoning.[43] Given that virtually every person lacks something in the way of knowledge and power, it is doubtful that any choice is fully voluntary. Nevertheless, this does not make it impossible for us to distinguish between nearly fully voluntary choices and those that are nearly involuntary. So, for example, it is possible to distinguish between a half-starved, teenaged runaway who "decides" to be a prostitute, and a well-fed, adult preprofessional who becomes a high-class call girl in order to make a lot of money very quickly. In the former case, most persons are inclined to think that the state may intervene, at least temporarily, for the teenager's own good. In the latter case, however, many persons are inclined to think otherwise, observing that a competent, well-informed, calm, mature, unconstrained, full-grown woman is the best judge of her own good.

But even if it is morally acceptable to risk one's own life and limb, provided that one's decision to do so is fully or nearly fully voluntary, it is not necessarily morally acceptable to risk other persons' lives, limbs, or general welfare in the process of doing so. When a Jehovah's Witness refuses a much-needed blood transfusion, her decision affects not only herself, but her survivors, her insurance company, her creditors, and her society. Indeed, this is why the state will force any Jehovah's Witness—male or female—to have a needed transfusion if he or she is a single parent unable to make provisions for the care of his or her orphaned children. The right of Jehovah's Witnesses to practice their religion is tempered by the obligations they assume when they decide to be fruitful and multiply. The situation is even more complicated, however, when involuntary risks are imposed on significant numbers of the population by voluntary risk takers (smoking comes to mind) or when involuntary risks are imposed on the populace as a whole by policymakers. Not all of us have the wherewithal to move on simply because the government decides to build a nuclear reactor close to our home or to find another job simply because an industry decides to build a polluting factory next to our place of employment. Thus, the risk-benefit analyst must devise techniques that can accommodate not only the differences between voluntary risks and involuntary risks, but also between personal risks that affect only oneself and personal risks that affect others. On the face of it, it is morally unacceptable to put people at risk, especially if the imposed risk promises them no benefits or "benefits" they would prefer to forsake.

Argument 3 Countered. Finally, Shrader-Frechette argues that it is not necessarily morally acceptable to risk what Rasmussen and others term a "significantly insignificant" number of induced deaths in exchange for considerable economic benefits.[44] Like Alasdair MacIntyre, she believes that risk-benefit analysis suffers from what many ethicists identify as the fatal flaw of utilitarianism, namely, a willingness to sacrifice individual rights for aggregate utility. A close reading of Shrader-Frechette suggests, however, that she is not an absolutist who believes that no increase in utility—no matter how large and no matter how carefully supported by risk-benefit analysis—is worth risking a single human life. Taken to this extreme, the absolutist position would force us to ban many life-risking technologies that have added to the quality of human life. To help us appreciate the fact that we are all risk takers, Earl MacCormac asks us to situate ourselves on a spectrum of risk that ranges from a position in a very low risk society where only the bare necessities for survival—food, shelter, defense against animals—are provided, to a position in "a complex technological society of great culture and enjoyment but also extremely high risk of extinction of human life through the existence of 50,000 nuclear weapons.[45] How many of us would decide to exist on the low end of this spectrum? On the high end? Somewhere in between? Assuming that we will sort ourselves out along this spectrum, how are policymakers to decide how much low-level radiation or pollution, for example, is too much?

Conclusion. Like cost-benefit analysis, risk-benefit analysis needs to be refined before we are able to assess risks to our satisfaction. Unfortunately, even if risk-benefit analysts perfect the science of risk *estimation*, I doubt that they will ever be able to perfect the art of risk *acceptance*. What makes a risk morally acceptable is its reasonability. According to Joel Feinberg, there are at least five considerations that enable us to distinguish a reasonable from an unreasonable risk:

> (1) the degree of probability that harm to oneself will result from a given course of action, (2) the seriousness of the harm being risked, i.e., "the value or importance of that which is exposed to the risk," (3) the degree of probability that the goal inclining one to shoulder the risk will in fact result from the course of action, (4) the value or importance of achieving that goal, that is, just how worthwhile it is to one (this is the intimately personal factor, requiring a decision about one's own preferences, that makes it so difficult for the outsiders to judge the reasonableness of a risk), and (5) the necessity of the risk, that is, the availability or absence of alternative, less risky, means to the desired goal.[46]

Feinberg is, of course, thinking in terms of an individual person who must decide, for example, whether cigarette smoking is a reasonable risk for a middle-aged man to assume. Nevertheless, what Feinberg says applies equally well to a group of persons, for example, who must decide whether or not it is reasonable for them to site a nuclear reactor in their midst.

Not all judgments about the reasonableness of a risk assumption will be controversial. Some will be noncontroversial. For example, if no alternatives to inexpensive energy other than nuclear energy are available, and if the chances of serious harm befalling the town of Billsville are small, and if it seems very likely that a nuclear reactor will generate inexpensive energy for townspeople's homes and industries, then it seems reasonable to site a nuclear reactor in Billsville. But what decision should the inhabitants of another community—call it Janesville—make if the probability of serious harm befalling them is considerable, but their need for inexpensive energy is desperate? Should they cast caution to the winds? Seemingly, the reasonableness of a risk has much to do with the value of achieving a given goal. Whereas the inhabitants of one town may prefer poorly heated homes and the shutdown of all its industries to a riskful existence, the inhabitants of another town may prefer warmly heated homes and thriving industries to a risk-free existence. It is this "intimately personal factor," involving a ranking of subjective preferences, that makes it so difficult, claims Feinberg, for one person or group to judge whether or not another person or group is being reasonable when it assumes a risk.[47] Therefore, unless we develop criteria to distinguish between reasonable and unreasonable preferences—a most difficult task—risk-benefit analysis will remain a useful tool for analyzing the probability but not the acceptability of risks.

PARADIGMS FOR THE POST-POSTIVIST POLICY EXPERT

What a critique and defense of cost-benefit analysis and risk-benefit analysis show, I believe, is the degree to which policy experts are rethinking the relationship between fact and value, and the extent to which the positivist world view is passé.

Every year fewer policy experts classify themselves as mere technicians who are concerned only with the skills and tools of their trade and who eschew politics. Arnold
Meltsner, author of *Policy Analysts in the Bureaucracy*, reports that contemporary
policy experts generally classify themselves either as "politicians" who enjoy the
opportunity to gain a broad perspective on public policy or as "entrepreneurs"
whose central occupational motivation is the desire to use analysis and advice not
as an end in itself but as a means to influence policy decisions.[48] In a related vein,
if my interviews of 25 Washington, D.C., policy analysts, advisers, and consultants
were at all representative, then a growing number of policy experts believe that
their occupational world is inhabited not by pure facts but by value-laded facts and
fact-laden values. Comments one science consultant:

> I don't believe that there are experts who come to problems without values.
> This may happen occasionally, but I don't think that I can ever remember it
> happening. I would point out that science itself is a value. Science basically
> assumes that the world is rational, and this is a value (indeed it is an act of
> faith). In this connection, let me raise the example of the ozone-freon contro-
> versy which came to light around 1975. The scientists predicted that freons—
> through complicated photochemical reactions—would destroy the stratos-
> pheric ozone layer protecting the Earth from ultraviolet light. They made this
> prediction on the basis of laboratory experiments extrapolated, as it were,
> into the strateosphere by means of computer models. This was a good exam-
> ple of belief in the rationality of the universe. It was clear to them that
> destruction of the ozone layer (1) would happen, and (2) would be a bad
> thing. Needless to say, the manufacturers of freons whose markets would
> have been impacted by a resulting ban on their use and manufacture did not
> see things exactly the same way. The point is not science versus business;
> rather the point is that the scientists became advocates for their "scientific"
> point of view. They argued strenuously in favor of their position and used the
> "facts" at their disposal to support their argument. The scientists did not feel
> an obligation to consider the question of employment in the freon industry,
> the question of the beneficial uses of freons, etc. (For example, it seems clear
> to me that the public health impact of an immediate and total ban on the use
> of freons would have been catastrophic because of the degree to which we
> depend on them for refrigeration of our food supplies). It turns out now that
> the very complicated models used to predict ozone destruction were not as
> accurate as some believed at the time, and the destruction of the ozone may
> not be quite as disastrous as we had thought.[49]

What is most remarkable about this consultant's statement is that it is very like the
statements made by the other 24 experts I interviewed. Each of them shared a
similar general view, reinforcing it with their own specific examples.

   This growing awareness on the part of policy analysts of the complicated inter-
relations among their epistemological assumptions, political commitments, and
ethical beliefs manifests itself in the way these men and women approach the discharge of their perceived moral duties. Although these approaches are many and
varied, they sort themselves out into three categories: (1) those that encouarge
policy experts to develop moral positions and to espouse political causes, but out-

side the work place; (2) those that encourage policy experts to speak the language of ethics as well as the language of technics in the work place; and (3) those that encourage policy experts not only to understand that ethics, politics, and epistemology are always and everywhere intertwined, but also to make this clear to all who seek their analysis and advice. Here I discuss each of these approaches in order of their ascending radicality, arguing that the third, if accepted, best enables us to weave moral values into the fabric of public policy.

Approach I

Among the most guarded approaches to the underscoring of moral concerns among policy experts is that of Edward Shils. Shils is not prepared to abandon the idea of the neutral fact. For him, the fact-value distinction is not merely a conceptual distinction but also a reflection of reality. What enables the policy expert to provide objective analysis and advice is the belief that there is something outside the truth seeker's own subjectivity to which he or she owes not so much a "moral" as a "cognitive" obligation. Comments Shils:

> For the scientist there are the facts of his observation, for a scholar there are the facts of his text, inscriptions, and monuments. They are the fragments of the external, objectively existing world to which the cognitive obligation is due and between and behind those fragments is the external, objectively existing world into which the fragments must be fitted.[50]

Despite his allegiance to the facts and to what they represent (truth or reality), Shils believes that policy experts ought to have an outlet for their moral and political concerns. Although policy analysts and advisers must not let their values direct, distort, or discredit their work, they can and ought to be sensitive to the ethical and political implications of their work. In *The Calling of Sociology*, Shils reminds his readers that while Max Weber was observing the highest standards of macrosociological analysis in the composition of some of his greatest works (*Hinduismus und Buddhismus, Das antike Judentum* and *Wirtschaft und Gesell-schaft*), he was simultaneously writing impassioned polemics against German imperial policy and the conduct of the First World War. As Shils sees it, provided that policy experts are aware of their political, religious, ethnic, and cultural "biases," "interests," and "background assumptions," and provided that they, *as scientists and technicians*, bracket these "values" so that they can expose "the facts," they not only may but should hold on to and express their convictions *as citizens* or simply as *moral agents*.[51]

Approach II

What is ultimately disappointing about Shils's position is that it lends credence to the positivist view according to which values are unamenable to rational discourse. Supposedly, people *emote* values; they cannot *reason* about them as they can reason about facts. Convinced that ethical and political values are no less amenable to rational discourse than scientific facts, Duncan MacRae and others argue against Shils that policy analysts and advisers ought to bring their "biases," "interests," and "background assumptions" to work. It bothers MacRae that value-oriented policy experts are frequently cautioned by their fact-ruled peers and superiors to "cool it" in one of several ways: (1) by working for a political group like the Nuclear Freeze Movement on their day off; (2) by seeking full-time employment at organizations—presumably second-rate—whose values coincide with their own; and/or (3) by writing value-laden scholarly articles on topics related to the soft "underbelly," though not to the hard core, of their respective disciplines.[52]

Although MacRae admits that any one of these courses of action is better than doing nothing, he believes that what politically and ethically sensitive policy experts really want is the regular opportunity to discuss the values that either implicitly or explicitly guide their everyday work. MacRae suggests that the way to introduce normative discourse into the workplace is to make formal provisions for its routine insertion. Suppose that a policymaker asks two policy experts to do a risk-benefit analysis in order to determine whether a nuclear power plant should be constructed at a certain site. One possible outcome is that policy analyst X and policy analyst Y come out with diametrically opposed recommendations, not because one of them has forgotten to factor in risks like the probability of a core meltdown or because one of them has ignored the benefits of inexpensive energy, but because both of them believe that a risk-benefit analysis includes both the estimation of risk and the determination of its acceptability. Precisely because policy analyst X believes that the economic and technological benefits gained by allowing some radioactivity to be dispersed in the environment are worth an increase in cancer and genetic damage, he will argue that the benefits associated with the production of nuclear energy far outweigh its risks. Similarly, precisely because policy analyst Y believes that the risks associated with the production of nuclear energy impact differentially on adults and children—children are from three to six times more likely than adults to contract cancer because of exposure to the maximum permissible annual dose of low-level radiation—she will argue that the economic and technological benefits gained by radioactivity-dispersing nuclear power do not automatically override or make acceptable the trumping of those of our "cultural norms" that "follow the Fifth and Fourteenth Amendment, and are based on concepts of equal justice, equal protection, and due process for all."[53]

Now it could be argued *àla* Shils that policy experts have no business letting their ethical biases enter into their analyses. But it is hard to imagine how ethics can always be bracketed from technics. If "risk acceptability" is as much a part of risk-benefit analysis as "risk estimation," then ethics is an equal partner with technics. Moreover, unless our two analysts share their moral assumptions with the policymaker for when they work, he or she might mistake ethics for technics or vice versa. Worse, the policymaker might be deprived of an opportunity to consider which risks may be legitimately imposed upon citizens. For all these reasons, when ethics and technics insist on merging together, MacRae urges policymakers to listen to their policy experts engage in a debate governed by three formal rules:

1. Ethical argument is to be conducted between the proponents of ethical systems that are specified in writing in advance.
2. Each discussant shall have equal opportunity to argue for his own system, and against the opposing one, by pointing out presumed shortcomings in the other system.
   a. Lack of generality.
   b. Internal inconsistency.
   c. Inconsistency with presumably shared moral convictions.
3. After each such opportunity to present conflict situations, the proponent of the ethical system under criticism shall decide whether he wishes to alter his ethical system or to make the choice dictated by it.[54]

Provided that our two policy analysts adhere to these rules, thus presenting their conflicting moral points of view in a rational manner, MacRae assures us that the policymaker who employs them will be in a position to decide whether or not the public is best served by the construction of a nuclear power plant in its midst.

Approach III

Although MacRae brings values and facts closer together, he still views normative discourse as merely complementary and not integral to the ways in which scientific disciplines accumulate and use knowledge. For him, values are the icing on the policy expert's cake. MacRae does not believe, as do more radical critics of positivism, that values are mixed directly into the policy batter, accounting for its sweet or bitter taste. In contrast, Jürgen Habermas argues that insofar as our experience is concerned, fact is just as inseparable from value as form is from matter. In the same way that we never encounter pure form or pure matter, we never encounter pure facts or pure values. The policy world is populated neither by pure factors nor by pure values, but by value-laden facts. Somewhat more controversially, Habermas also argues that, more often than not, facts are selected by values. What he means by this cryptic saying is that human interests determine what counts as a relevant fact. Supposedly, humans have three types of fundamental interests: (1) an interest in controlling the natural environment; (2) an interest in communication, that is, mutual understanding and joint enterprise in a context of common social traditions; and (3) an interest in emancipation, that is, an interest in becoming free of ideological mystification and enslaving social constraints. These three interests guide the process of inquiry in which data, or facts, are collected for three corresponding forms of knowledge: the empirical-analytical sciences, the historical-hermeneutical sciences, and the critical sciences such as psychoanalysis.[55] If, for example, humans had not been interested in controlling nature, the natural sciences as we know them today would be nonexistent. Certainly, in the absence of a human interest in understanding the composition of the material universe, something like the atom would never have been separated out from that "bloomin' buzzin' confusion"[56] that renders invisible that in which no one has an interest. Scientists discovered atoms, suggests Habermas, because they were looking for them.

As a result of Habermas's explanation of the complex interplay between fact and value, positivistic policy science is losing ground to what is termed the "interpretive" approach to policy science. Bruce Jennings, one of the leading exponents of this new approach, argues that interpretive policy science differs from positivistic policy science in several crucial respects. First, whereas positivistic policy science prides itself on its fidelity to empiricism and its army of docile, neutral facts, interpretive policy science defiantly claims that facts are neither docile nor neutral. On the contrary, they are all unruly (essentially contestable) and value-laden (interpreted). To say that interpretive policy science rejects empiricism, however, is not to say that it rejects empirical analysis. Empiricism is an epistemological doctrine; empirical analysis is a mode of inquiry. The question raised by interpretive policy science is not whether facts are relevant to empirical analysis, but what kind of facts are selected and how they are to be interpreted. Similarly, to say that interpretive policy science rejects neutral facts and focuses instead on interpreted facts is not to say that all interpretations are equally valid, thereby plunging us into irrationality and subjectivism. Rather it is to look "more closely at how standards of judgment operate and are developed in the humanistic disciplines, such as historical narrative, ethical argument, literary exegesis, and jurisprudential reasoning," and to ascertain whether these standards promise more guidance to the policy sciences than do the norms of the natural and social sciences.[57] Second, whereas success in positivistic policy science depends only on the analyst's technical training, success in interpretive policy science also depends on the insight and creativity of the analyst. Unlike the positivistic policy scientist, the interpretive policy scientist is not content to study the mere fact that x did y and under what conditions x is likely to do y again. Rather, he or she also wants to know why x decided to do y and how y is related to x's past activities. Thus, the interpretive policy scientist aims to explain human activities, social relationships, and cultural artifacts in terms of an agent's reasons for doing an action, establishing a relationship, or making an artifact. In turn, these reasons are explained in terms of the context of conventions, rules, and norms within which they are formed. Unlike the positivistic policy scientist who moves from the specific to the general in order to subsume particular events under universal laws, the interpretive policy scientist does not "move up and down a ladder." Rather he or she "spins a web," explaining the meaning of a given activity, relationship, or artifact in an ever-widening web of interrelated activities, relationships, and artifacts. Third and finally, whereas positivistic policy science is generally a mere matter of generating statistics, enumerating facts, and cataloging information, interpretive policy science is also a rhetorical or persuasive medium. Facts do not speak for themselves. The interpretive analyst must speak on their behalf.[58]

CONCLUSION

If the preceding comparisons and contrasts are largely accurate, then for policymakers and policy experts to opt for interpretive policy analyses over positivistic policy analyses is for them to decide that a reconstruction of the processes of practical reasoning is a more useful basis for making policy than deductive-nomological causal explanations and predictions. In this connection, Robert Bellah sets up a contrast between what he calls "technical" and "practical" policy science. This distinction, which echoes Jennings's distinction between positivistic and interpretive policy science, is rooted in Aristotle's contrast between *techne* and *praxis* as it is developed in the *Nicomachean Ethics*. For Aristotle, technical reason (*techne*) is the process whereby the artisan molds matter into a preconceived product. In contrast, practical reason (*praxis*) has no product over and beyond itself. The process of ethical and political reflection is its own end.[59] In other words, in and through communal thinking and speaking, a group of people, intent on doing the good, become good whether or not their actions actually achieve their intended objectives. The best-laid plans of mice and men may fail in the sense that a battle, for example, is not won after all. But provided that a hodgepodge of disparate individuals with competing wants and needs have become one in their efforts to forge the best possible communal policy their limited knowledge and power permits, such plans will not have failed in a more ultimate sense.

As Bellah sees it, a technical policy science is "proud." It promises a genuine science of human behavior on the model of modern natural sciences, true in all possible worlds, and in order to make good on its promise, it produces instruments toward the *understanding* of society by external observers. Policy experts, who view themselves merely as technicians, tend to set themselves over against the "objects" of their inquiry. They are prone to follow the advice of persons like sociologist Robert Park, who used to advise race-relations students to approach their study of Black-White tensions "with the same objectivity and detachment with which the zoologist dissects the potato bug."[60] In contrast, a practical policy science is "humble." It does not promise the scientific precision to which technical policy science aspires, and it produces instruments toward the *self-understanding* of society by those who live, move, and have their being in it. Policy experts, who view themselves not so much as technicians but as persons intent on exercising their powers of practical reason, do not set themselves up against the "objects" they study. They are smart enough to know the differences between a person and a potato bug, and wise enough to realize that technical knowledge is only one rather fallible input into a complex situation that also requires common sense, ethical insight, and a great deal of conversation with ordinary citizens and decision makers before a policy can be forged.

What I will argue in Chapter 3 is that the sooner all policy experts and policy-makers accept the limits of technical knowledge, the sooner they will be in a position to create with and for us a more democratic public policy. If Bruce Jennings is correct to posit a relationship between a style of discourse that describes human agents as casually determined objects and a form of government that relies on manipulation (e.g., behavior control) for the achievement of externally imposed social objectives and the maintenance of social order,[62] then we may also be correct to posit a relationship between a style of discourse that describes human agents as self-determining subjects and a form of government that relies on the informed participation of those agents for the achievement of mutually agreed-upon social objectives and the maintenance not of mere social order but of true human community. Thus, while it is true to say that our politics and ethics affect our epistemology, it is equally true to day that our epistemology—broadly conceived as our vision of reality—affects our politics and yes, our ethics.

NOTES

1. David Held, *Introduction to Critical Theory: Horkheimer to Habermas* (Berkeley: University of Californa Press, 1980), 163–64.

2. Joel Primack and Frank von Hippel, *Advice and Dissent: Scientists in the Political Arena* (New York: Basic Books, Inc., Publishers, 1974) 7.

3. Freeman Dyson, *Disturbing the Universe* (New York: Harper Colophon Books, 1979) 52.

4. Martin Tolchim, "Regulation and the Economist," *New York Times*, 20 Nov. 1983, sec. F, 4.

5. Vincent Vacarro, "Cost Benefit Analysis and Public Policy Formulation," in *Ethical Issues in Government*, ed. Norman Bowie (Philadelphia, Temple University Press, 1981) 156–59.

6. Ida R. Hoos, *Systems Analysis in Public Policy: A Critique* (Berkeley: University of California Press, 1972), 25.

7. Ibid., 141.

8. Ibid.

9. Ibid., 145.

10. Alasdair MacIntyre, "Utilitarianism and Cost/Benefit Analysis: An Essay on the Relevance of Moral Philosophy to Bureaucratic Theory," in *Ethical Theory and Business*, eds. Tom L. Beauchamp and Norman E. Bowie (Englewood Cliffs, N.J.: Prentice-Hall, Inc., 1979), 268.

11. Ibid., 270.

12. Ibid., 271–74.

13. Tom L. Beauchamp, "The Moral Adequacy of Cost-Benefit Analysis as the Basis for Government Regulation of Research," and Vacarro, "Cost-Benefit Analysis and Public Policy Formulation," in *Ethical Issues in Government*, ed. Bowie, 163–76 and 146–63, respectively.

14. Vacarro, "Cost-Benefit Analysis and Public Policy Formulation," 149.

15. Burton A. Weisbrod, "Appendix A: Concepts of Costs and Benefits," in *Problems in Public Expenditure Analysis*, ed. Samuel B. Chase (Washington, D.C.: Brookings Institution, 1968), 257–62.

16. MacIntyre, "Utilitarianism and Cost-Benefit Analysis," 272.

17. Steven E. Rhoads, "How Much Should We Spend to Save a Life?" in *Valuing Life: Public Policy Dilemmas*, ed. Steven E. Rhoads (Boulder, Colo.: Westview Press, 1980), 290. Reprinted by permission of Westview Press. Copyright © 1980 by Westview Press, Boulder, CO.

18. Ibid., 291. Here Rhoads points out that "the WTP approach does not focus on how much people would pay to avoid certain death, for in such a situation most people would pay almost all they could get their hands on, and thus the WTP figure would reveal more about absolute wealth than about the relative preference for a particular good or service."

19. Ibid.

20. R. Coburn, "Technology Assessment, Human Good, and Freedom," in *Ethics and Problems of the 21st Century*, eds. K. E. Goodpaster and K. M. Sayre (Notre Dame, Ind.: University of Notre Dame Press, 1979), 109.

21. Kristin S. Shrader-Frechette, "Technology Assessment as Applied Philosophy of Science," *Science, Technology and Human Values*, 6, no. 33 (Fall 1980) 39.

22. Coburn, "Technology Assessment, Human Good, and Freedom," p. 109.

23. Rhoads, "How Much Should We Spend to Save a Life?" in *Valuing Life*, ed. Rhoads, 299–300.

24. Ibid., 300.

25. Immanuel Kant, *Foundations of the Metaphysics of Morals*, (New York: Bobbs-Merrill Company, Inc., 1959), p. 41.

26. Vacarro, "Cost-Benefit Analysis and Public Policy Formulation," 151.

27. Shrader-Frechette, "Technology Assessment as Applied Philosophy of Science," p. 38.

28. Herman B. Leonard and Richard J. Zeckhauser, "Cost-Benefit Analysis Defended," *Philosophy and Public Policy* 3, no. 3 (Summer 1983), 6.

29. Ibid.

30. Shrader-Frechette, "Technology Assessment as Applied Philosophy of Science," p. 35.

31. E. L. Quade, *Analysis for Public Decisions* (New York: American Elsevier Publishing Co., Inc., 1975), 26.

32. U.S. Congress, OTA, *The Direct Use of Coal* (Washington, D.C.: U.S. Government Printing Office, 1979), pp. 316–34.

33. Sheldon S. Wolin, "The New Public Philosophy," *Democracy* 1, no. 4 (October 1981), 29.

34. Ibid.

35. William D. Rowe, "Introduction to Risk Assessment," in *Energy Risk Management* (New York: Academic Press, 1979), 8–10.

36. Raphael G. Kasper, "'Real' Versus Perceived Risk: Implications for Policy," in ibid., 88.

37. L. Rasmussen, ed., "Reactor Safety Study: An Assessment of Accident Risks in U.S. Commercial Nuclear Power Plants," Report, WASH-1400, U.S. Nuclear Regulation Commission, 1975.

38. K. S. Shrader-Frechette, *Nuclear Power and Public Policy* (Dordrecht, Holland: D. Reidel Publishing Company, 1980), 83–84.

39. Joel Primack and Frank von Hippel, "Nuclear Reactor Safety," *The Bulletin of the Atomic Scientists* 30, no. 8 (October 1974), 7–9.

40. Shrader-Frechette, *Nuclear Power and Public Policy*, 87.

41. Ibid., 140.

42. Ibid., 143.

43. Joel Feinberg, *Social Philosophy* (Englewood Cliffs, N.J.: Prentice-Hall, Inc., 1973), 48.

44. Shrader-Frechette, *Nuclear Power and Public Policy*, 149.

45. Earl L. MacCormac, "Values and Technology: How to Introduce Ethical and Human Values into Public Policy Decisions" (Unpublished paper, 1982), 5.

46. Feinberg, *Social Philosophy*, 47.

47. Ibid., 47–48.

48. Arnold J. Meltsner, *Policy Analysts in the Bureaucracy* (Berkeley: University of California Press, 1976), 48.

49. Interview with an anonymous Washington, D.C., science consultant.

50. Edward Shils, *The Calling of Sociology and Other Essays on the Pursuit of Learning* (Chicago: The University of Chicago Press, 1980), 366–67.

51. Ibid., 415.

52. Duncan MacRae, Jr., *The Social Function of Social Science* (New Haven, Conn. Yale University Press, 1976), 72.

53. Shrader-Frechette, *Nuclear Power and Public Policy*, p. 35.

54. Ibid., 90–92.

55. Held, *Introduction to Critical Theory*, 296–324.

56. Thomas Kuhn, *The Structure of Scientific Revolutions* (Chicago: University of Chicago Press, 1962), 113.

57. Bruce Jennings, "Interpretive Social Science and Policy Analysis," in *Ethics, the Social Sciences and Policy Analysis*, eds. Daniel Callahan and Bruce Jennings (New York: Plenum Press, 1983), 19.

58. Ibid., 12–16.

59. Robert N. Bellah, "Social Science as Practical Reason," in *Ethics, the Social Sciences and Policy Analysis*, eds. Callahan and Jennings, 43.

60. E. W. Burgess, "Social Planning and Race Relations," in *Race Relations Problems and Theories*, ed. by J. Masvoka and P. Valien (Chapel Hill, N.C.: University of North Carolina Press, 1961), 17.

61. Bellah, "Social Science as Practical Reason," in ibid., 63–64.

62. Jennings, "Interpretive Social Science and Policy Analysis," 34.

Chapter 3

The Role of the Expert
in a Democratic Society

As Marshall Berman has noted, this age is decisively set off from earlier ones by the industrialization of production, demographic upheavals, cataclysmic urban growth, mass-communication systems, mass social movements, and an ever-expanding drastically fluctuating capitalist work market.[1] Of all these changes, however, none is more dramatic than the communications or knowledge explosion, and the growing dependence of policymakers on specially created knowledge. Today, large-scale bureaucratic enterprises—especially the government—rely on endless streams of new data in order to back their power, to pursue ever more complex goals, and to forge comprehensive public policies. These data do not rain down upon Washingtonians as the manna rained down upon the Israelites of old, however. Rather they are distilled from the sweat of experts—from the brows of natural, social and policy scientists who serve as analysts, advisers, and consultants. And given that this is a highly complicated and conflicted society, those with the truth, the scientific and technical experts, tend to roar rather than to whisper their advice to those with the official power.[2]

But if scientific truth is just as perspectival as ethical truth, then what we see depends not only on what we look at, but also on what our "previous visual-conceptual experience" has taught us to see. Absent such tutoring, there can only be a perceptual morass of indistinguishable entities.[3] Like all mortals, policy analysts and advisers are burdened with their peculiar perspectives. They come from Brookings, the American Enterprise Institute, or the Hoover Institution; from small elite colleges, large state universities, or big business; and they bring to the national capital their political and ethical baggage as well as their trade tools. Whether we like it or not, we must rely upon these experts for assurance that nuclear weapons and nuclear reactors will not explode accidentally; that the people who need welfare services will not be deprived of them; that adequate fuel will be available to keep us warm, moving, and employed; that the chemicals we add to our food and water supplies will not poison us; and so on. And whether we like it or not, the way in which experts make their services available to society can significantly affect the distribution of political power. If, on the one hand, policy scientists give government and industry the exclusive benefit of their expertise, they may inadvertently contribute to the creation of a technocracy in which we relatively uninformed types must accept whatever those in power tell us is in our best interest. If, on the other hand, these same experts directly communicate to us the information we need for the defense of our health and welfare, they can help bring about more open and democratic controls in the uses of science and technology.

Considerations such as these require us to scrutinize the roles policy experts play in a democratic society. Among these roles are those of policy analyst, subject-area specialist, and policy adviser. Of these roles, that of policy analyst is probably the most specified, although it is not always possible to distinguish a policy analyst from either a subject-area specialist or a policy adviser.

Policy analysis came into its own when policymakers were pressed to answer the moon-ghetto problem: "If we can land a man on the moon, why can't we solve the problems of the ghetto?"[4] A new breed of whiz kids answered that we would never be able to solve problems like that of the ghetto until policymakers had the best information available at their disposal. Supposedly, the surest way to obtain this data base was for policymakers to hire a slew of analysts able to generate rational and objective assessments of costs, benefits, and alternatives. Hired en masse and armed primarily with the weapons of the economist—notably, the calculative structures of operations research, systems analysis, cost-effectiveness analysis, cost-benefit analysis, and risk-benefit analysis—policy analysts proceeded to produce the hoped-for assessments. No sooner did they publish their findings, however, than they found themselves in conflict with subject-area specialists in the fields they were analyzing —doctors regarding health matters, generals regarding defense matters, social workers regarding welfare matters, and teachers regarding education matters.

In some instances, the specialists simply complained "that the analysts didn't know how the system really worked, and that their [the analysts'] models were drastically over simplified."[5] In other instances the specialists expressed considerable distress over the fact that their values were fundamentally at odds with those of the analysts'. Ida Hoos cites a hypothetical case in point. A college could hire a team of analysts to construct a cost model relating each of several disciplines respectively to such expenses as faculty salaries, support-staff salaries, square feet of space occupied, overhead and upkeep costs, and so on. Predictably, the model demonstrates the "obvious"; namely,

> that high-energy physics, with a small number of students per class, high faculty-student ratio, enormous need for space for accelerators, peripheral apparatus, laboratories, extremely expensive computers, and other equipment, [shows] relatively low "output," calculated in number of graduates and their employment under conditions of severe retrenchment in science.[6]

Faced with such data, the typical policy analyst is likely to suggest solutions like cutting back enrollments in high-energy physics, reducing faculty salaries, denying requests for the purchase of state-of-the-art equipment, and so on. In contrast, the typical academic is likely to argue that certain subjects, no matter how costly in terms of dollars, must remain in the curriculum both to remind us all that the pursuit of truth per se is valuable and to attract the best and the brightest to academia.[7] Thus, observes Hoos, the commissioners of the study are left to choose between two incommensurable paradigms. Or are they?

Ten to fifteen years ago the type of paradigm conflict described above nearly always led, if not to a stalemate, then to one very unhappy group of experts. Today such no-win situations are less routine, and this is because subject-area specialists and policy analysts are beginning to appreciate each other's virtues as well as vices. Rather than fighting City Hall, so to speak, today's policy analysts are not only more willing to accept subject-area specialists as their intellectual equals, but to regard themselves as specialists. If nothing more, the advantages of combining in one person the skills of the analyst and the insights of the subject-area specialist meet the requirements of old-fashioned common sense.[8] To hire someone trained in prison reform as a Treasury policy analyst is a waste of time and energy if someone trained in public finance is available. Obviously someone who already knows about the concepts of equity, tax shifting, progressivity of taxes, and fiscal neutrality is better equipped to work for the Treasury Department than a prison-reform specialist who has to have her income tax forms filled out by H & R Block. Unfortunately, common sense as well as the right person for the job are sometimes in short supply. We still find engineers working on child-health problems and medical doctors working on organizational questions.[9] Although analysts can perform well even under such non-optional conditions, they usually perform better when their policy area meshes with their educational background.

To the degree that the roles of the policy analyst and the subject-area specialist are increasingly indiscernable, so too is it more and more difficult to articulate how a policy adviser differs from a policy analyst or a policy specialist. Initially, this may strike some readers as an exaggeration. Ordinarily, when we think of an adviser we are not likely to think of an analyst or specialist who performs nuts-and-bolts operations like computer programming, poll taking, or library research. Rather we are apt to point to someone newsworthy like the reigning Science Adviser or the current luminary in the Office of Economic Advisers. Admittedly, such thinking is not purely speculative. Not all analysts, specialists, and advisers play an equal role in the policymaking process. Nevertheless, to construct a rigid caste system among these three types is to misrepresent the complexity and fluidity of the policy hierarchy. Upon careful reflection, it seems that the policy analyst or subject-area specialist in the bowels of the bureaucracy is, to some degree, a policy adviser, and that the policy adviser at the top of the bureaucracy is, to some degree, nothing other than an analyst or specialist.

Among those who insist that even the lowest-ranking policy analyst is in some sense an adviser is Arnold Meltsner.[10] As Meltsner sees it, policymakers are as likely to go to a staff analyst for advice as to a spouse, a trusted confidant, a prestigious academician, or a Joint Chief of Staff.[11] In a similar vein, but focusing instead on the high-level policy adviser, Herbert Goldhamer points out that advisers have performed analytical tasks for centuries.[12] He traces operations research back at least as far as Han Fei Tzu (circa 300 B.C.), and he quotes the advice of Erasmus to "take a rational estimate long enough to reckon what the war will cost and whether the final end to be gained is worth that much."[13] Any attempt to claim, for example, that the business of analysts is simply analysis and that the concern of advisers is simply advice is likely to be met with skepticism on Goldhamer's part. As far as he can determine, analysts are always advising and advisers are always analyzing.

Since policy analysts, subject-area specialists, and policy advisers apparently share many functions in common, I will in this and subsequent chapters feel free to discuss problems that plague any one or all of these groups. In the main, this chapter will address a question that has yet to be answered satisfactorily: Is rule by an educated elite to be preferred to rule by the uneducated masses, or is majority rule more valuable than the material benefits that the minds of the few can purchase for the bodies of many? In this connection, we will discuss (1) the transition from ethics to politics and finally to technics as the dominant discourse, (2) the ongoing battle between elitists on the one hand and exponents of representative and/or participatory democracy on the other hand, and (3) the "demoralization" of citizens by experts.

THE EFFECT OF EXPERTISE ON CULTURE:
ETHICS, POLITICS, AND TECHNICS
AS COMPETING DISCOURSES

In his classic article, "The Decline of Politics and Ideology in a Knowledgeable Society," Robert E. Lane describes contemporary society as one in which, more than in other societies, its members:

1. Inquire into the basis of their beliefs about man, nature, and society;
2. Are guided (perhaps unconsciously) by objective standards of veridical truth, and, at the upper levels of education, follow scientific rules of evidence and inference in inquiry;
3. Denote considerable resources to this inquiry and thus have a large store of knowledge;
4. Collect, organize, and interpret their knowledge in a constant effort to extract further meaning from it for the purposes at hand;
5. Employ this knowledge to illuminate (and perhaps modify) their values and goals as well as to advance them.[14]

In support of this view, he notes, for example, that from 1940 to 1963 federal government expenditures for research and development increased from $74 million to $10 billion; that from 1950 to 1963 expenditures for research and development by colleges and universities increased from $420 million to $1.7 billion; and that in the seven years from 1957 to 1964 the number of Ph.D.'s conferred annually increased from 1,634 to 2,320 in the life sciences and from 1,824 to 2,860 in the social sciences.[15]

A principle consequence of growth in the direction of the knowledgeable society, Lane thinks, has been a shrinkage of the "political domain" (where decisions are the product of power struggles among people espousing disparate goals, all of which cannot be pursued) relative to the "knowledge domain" (where decisions are simply the rational and efficient implementation of already agreed-upon goals). Politics, Lane acknowledges, will not cease to exist even in the most knowledgeable of societies; but as our society becomes more knowledgeable, political debate will wane and scientific and technical jargon will wax.[16]

Significantly, the demise of politics and the ascendancy of technics is not met with universal enthusiasm. Some worry, for example, that the human community is losing something essential—namely, its political instincts and ethical vision—as scientific studies and technical analyses substitute for heated debates and extended conversations about the good, the true, and the beautiful. As we shall see, this concern is a real one. Nevertheless, provided that we realize how the language of technics affects our world view and our self-image, we may be able to control it for our purposes rather than simply succumbing to its imperatives.

The Transition from Ethics to Politics

In ancient times, ethics and politics were virtually indistinguishable. There were no distinctively political institutions (or scientific or economic institutions, for that matter) to reconcile with ethical beliefs, practices, and standards. The formulas for the good man and the good society were quite the same. For example, in Plato's *Republic* an isomorphic relationship exists between the virtues of the individual (wisdom, courage, temperance, and justice) and the virtues of the city. If all individual souls are rightly ordered, then society is rightly ordered, and vice versa. Plato's ideal state, as described in *The Republic*, and his second-best state, as schematized in *The Laws*, are both societies that have no political problems as we know them. Similarly, Aristotle's world is an amalgam of ethical and political considerations. For him, ethics and politics are two aspects of one path leading to the same good for man. When Aristotle says that man is by nature a political animal, he means that the distinctively human life—the life that marks us off from beasts and gods—is a life lived among fellow citizens, partners in virtue and friends in action. Such a life cannot be lived, however, in a society that fails to exercise practical reasoning because of an excessive, or even exclusive, reliance on technical reasoning.

On Aristotle's view, technical reasoning—the kind of reasoning involved in the production of health by the doctor, of a house by a builder, or of a missile by an engineer—can best be understood by distinguishing it from what it is not. First, technical reasoning is neither mere experience (mere familiarity with particular instances of production without insight into their universal principles of guidance) nor mere theory (knowledge of the abstract or universal without experiential acquaintance with the concrete or particular). Second, technical reasoning is not a "natural" but a "nonnatural" mode of production. Its logic is external rather than internal to that which it seeks to order. There is nothing *in* a pile of wood that says, "Build me into a house." Rather the builder sees a pile of wood and says, "I can fashion a house out of those bits and pieces of forest." Third, technical reasoning, which issues in production, is clearly other than practical reasoning, which issues in action.[17] That is to say, whereas the aim of technical reasoning is to control things —to mold matter to serve human purposes—the aim of practical reasoning is to liberate persons, to let them engage in those activities that will serve their best interests. An act is rational to the extent that it contributes to the mega-activity Aristotle terms *eudaimonia* (happiness or flourishing). Supposedly, we all share the ultimate goal of happiness or flourishing, and it is in terms of this goal that we assess our own and others' progress toward human excellence. To be rational is to be free of those external but especially internal forces that diminish our knowledge and power, thereby impeding our ability to act autonomously. In sum, the rational person is that person who not only knows but also is able and willing to do that which is *good* for one and all, for the one (the individual) is ultimately unhappy without the all (society).

In marked contrast to the classical tradition stands the modern tradition. Beginning with Machiavelli and culminating in the writings of Max Weber and Carl Schmitt, ethics is split off from politics. Machiavelli is the first political theorist to suggest that politics cannot always afford the luxury of ethics, that politicians can be too moral not only for their own good but for that of their people.[18] Thus Machiavelli instructs future princes to learn "how not to be good"[19] and how to get over the pangs of conscience on the way to establishing a powerful and prosperous state. By no means is Machiavelli's message lost on future generations. Writing in the nineteenth century, Max Weber points out that the person who is called to be a politician "lets himself in for the diabolic forces lurking in all violence."[20] Says Weber: "The genius or demon of politics lives in an inner tension with the god of love . . . . [which] can at any time lead to an irreconcilable conflict."[21] Both Machiavelli and Weber insist that the rules governing the public, or political, realm are different from the rules governing the private, or ethical, realm. As they see it, we cannot always accommodate both our political and our ethical values. Sometimes we have to make a hard choice between them.

Interestingly, it is the notion of competing values that dominates Carl Schmitt's thought. In place of the classical communitarian model, Schmitt offers a conflict model of social interaction. Not only must we sometimes choose between political and ethical values, oftentimes we must choose between two rival ethical values or between two rival political values. In the main, political life is not the process through which friends seek to live the same kind of good life together (think here of any intentional community); rather it is the process through which each person seeks to live his or her own particular good—to do his or her "own thing." Because this is so, Schmitt contends that the essential political distinction is that between friend and foe.[22] Thus, a person who has political sense is one who thinks about the opposition, and also about the support, actual and potential, that may be connected with any idea, activity, or institution. But even if this type of politics precludes classical communitarian ethics, it is not hostile to ethics broadly conceived. The healthier processes of conflict-oriented politics—bargaining, adjusting, adapting, compromising—have a moral dimension insofar as they require ordinary citizens to accept the consequences of their actions and to make ascriptions of responsibility.

The Transition from Politics to Technics

What is hostile to ethics, broadly or narrowly conceived, and ultimately to politics, be it based on a friendship model or a conflict model, however, is another modern stream of thought. Beginning with Hobbes, the message is communicated that we will not progress as individuals or as a species so long as we insist on regarding ourselves as controlling subjects rather than controllable objects. Hobbes observes that when human institutions "come to be dissolved" as a result of human error, "the fault is not in men, as they are the *matter* but as they are the *makers* "[24] of institutions. Hobbes paints a portrait of autonomous men as bungling clowns who, if they try to construct a sociopolitical order according to their own design, will construct "a crazy building, such as hardly lasting out their own time." The only hope for *homo stultus* is to hire a "very able architect" who will save him from his own worse impulses and incompetencies.[24]

What Hobbes is arguing here is not that different from what contemporary behaviorist B. F. Skinner says in his *Beyond Freedom and Dignity*. Skinner believes that the literature of freedom and dignity, with its concern for "autonomous man," is indirectly responsible for many of the woes that plague humankind. Because each of us thinks that we are in charge of our separate destinies, we weave a ragtag social quilt for each other. Were this quilt merely aesthetically displeasing, our situation would not be so perilous. But, as things stand, our group quilt is always on the verge of unraveling, since each of us individuals want to have it his or her own way.[25]

Skinner predicts that unless we give up the delusory role of controlling subject for the salutory role of controllable object, we will continue to create problems for ourselves. Given that we are nothing more than animate objects susceptible to the laws of psychology, biology, chemistry, and physics, we can largely avoid self-created problems by constructing a common environment whose constraints will enable us first to survive and then to thrive as a group. Skinner asks us to imagine a utopian world in which we all live together in peace and prosperity. We can have this world, believes Skinner, provided that we stop indulging our increasingly insatiable desire to do what we want, when we want, and how we want, and start marching instead to the disciplined beat of a common drummer.[26]

Anyone who believes that the psychic states of human persons, as well as their behavior, are completely determined by the interaction of their genes and environment will have no trouble with Skinner's utopia. If we are determined anyway, why not create a self and an environment for ourselves that will eliminate all the social evils that have plagued us so far? When the question is so phrased, there seems little, if any, reason not to jump into Skinner's box. But before we make this leap of faith, we had best give pause. If our thoughts and actions are as determined as the determinists insist, then we should think long and hard before we hand ourselves over to those who presumably know what environment to construct for us. Once we view our life together not as the struggle of each one of us to create a good life for all, but as the construction of a pleasure-producing environment for the many by the few, then politics no longer requires ethics. Gone are partners in virtue and friends in action. In their place stands a small scientific and technical elite that presumably discovers and delivers all the knowledge that is going to make life so easy for the masses. But what does this say about the masses? To put it crudely, it says that the masses are "lazy bums." To put it in at once more refined and obscuring terms, it says that while the "singularly talented few" will be playing an increasing role in decision making and continually updating their education and working overtime, the undistinguished many will be developing a new "interest in the cultural and humanistic aspects of life, *in addition to purely hedonistic preoccupations*."[27]

The problem with the masses engaging in wine, women (men?), and song from dawn to dusk, however, is that ordinary citizens lose any significant opportunity to participate in the policymaking process. Governmental choices cease to be expressions of a communal process of deliberation and become manifestations of the will of an elite coterie who speak a language comprehensible only to themselves.[28] In many ways this esoteric language, best termed technics, is what Latin was to the medieval peasantry: a mysterious jargon that permitted a small literate group of people to dominate the illiterate masses.[29] Ignorance, it seems, is not so much bliss as powerlessness.

Who Should Rule: The Elite Expert or the Common Man/Woman?

Americans' attitude towards experts have see-sawed back and forth from total admiration to complete scepticism to grudging respect. Immediately after World War II, for example, when the discoveries that led to Hiroshima were publicized, natural scientists were regarded as the ultimate authorities not only on the mysterious "bomb" but on all possible subjects. For a moment it seemed as if the philosopher-king had been reincarnated in the guise of physicist-king. Not only were post-Hiroshima physicists asked "to give simplified lectures on the nucleus to Congressional committees," they "were invited to conventions of social scientists where their opinions on society were respectfully listened to by life-long experts in the field."[30]

The Sputnik crisis intensified America's respect for and dependence upon the scientific community. Fearful lest their freedoms be devoured by the big "Red Bear," Americans gave natural scientists a virtual carte blanche with respect to their collective destiny. "Save us from the wicked foe, and you may do as you please." Interestingly, it was also in the late 1950s that adult Americans began to experience a general crisis in their ability to solve their own problems. Physically and/or mentally ill patients stopped curing themselves and started running to the doctors at the first sign of headache or depression; parents stopped using common sense and started to rely on Dr. Spock and his imitators; and troubled families stopped fighting "things" out and began discussing "matters" rationally in front of family counselors.

Challenging the Experts' Power

The Public's Fears. As a result of a series of scandals involving experts in the 1960s, however, the rule of the experts began to disassemble as rapidly as it had been assembled. Appalled by the participation of learned men and women in bio-chemical warfare, in health-hazard cover-ups, and in dubious social experiments, the American public began to lose faith in the best and the brightest. Moreover, challenged by books such as Ivan Illich's *Medical Nemesis* and Thomas Szasz's *The Myth of Mental Illness*, Americans began to question the advisability of ceding their responsibility for themselves to an army of experts. As a result of these two developments, experts were whittled down to size in the popular imagination and increasingly viewed either as corrupt opportunists or as arrogant "know-it-alls."

The Experts' Self-Doubt. Interestingly, the demythologization of experts has caused the experts themselves to reflect upon their proper role in a technological order that is also a democratic polity. Given that they are not elected representatives of the people, many experts wonder whether they overstep their authority by making values as well as facts their business. Ian Clark, for one, thinks that experts do exceed their authority on any occasion they wander into the realm of values. Clark claims that experts—be they policy analysts, subject-area specialists, or policy advisers—have but one proper role, that of technician: "Questions of policy can always be separated from technical questions. Experts should make this distinction explicit and should have no greater voice in the resolution of questions of policy than the ordinary citizen or layman."[31] Thus the expert ought to make the closest possible technical study of the matter at hand, allowing "the constitutionally determined government officials and politicians to make their choices among alternate policies."[32] Experts should offer facts and allow the policymakers and ultimately the citizens to choose values.

What Clark terms his "democratic paradigm" is seductive; after all, why should experts have any more say in policy decisions than ordinary citizens? For what reason do we elect members of Congress if they then cede their decision-making powers to private management consultants, "experts," and think tanks?[33] Yet Clark's paradigm is flawed. First, he simply takes it on faith that facts can be separated from values. But if we learned anything in Chapter 2, it is that it is probably easier to separate Siamese twins than it is to sever facts from values. Second, Clark does not explore the relationship between truth and power in any depth or detail. What we want to know, however, is whether the domain of politics can be kept safe from the control of an intellectual elite, whether the domain of science can be insulated from the blandishments of politics, and, ultimately, whether science and politics can work together for the people. It is to such considerations that we now turn.

Politics as It Is Threatened by Science

When we claim that science and technics are threatening politics, what we usually mean is that the idea of "responsible, responsive, representative government"[34] is losing its grip on our imagination. Because we are supposedly overwhelmed by scientific discoveries and technological devices, we are apparently disposed once again, as after World War II, not only to listen attentively to scientists and technicians but also to regard them increasingly as philosopher-kings and philosopher-queens whose superior knowledge entitles them to rule a populace incapable of governing itself wisely. But once we begin to view ourselves as less than self-controlling agents, we become has-been actors for whom politics is a silly charade: a purposeless game we play but only because we find it hard to relinquish totally our illusions of autonomy.[35]

What is particularly distressing about this devaluation of politics is that even purported defenders of democracy tend to sell democracy short. For example, although Don Price celebrates the separation of science and politics, and although he insists that an elaborate system of checks and balances is keeping order among what he describes as the four estates—the political estate, consisting of elected government officials; the administrative estate, consisting of managers and administrators in both government and private corporations; the professional estate, consisting of organized professionals who deal with the practical applications of scientific knowledge; and the scientific estate, consisting of scientists engaged in pure research—nevertheless, the world he sketches runs almost exclusively on scientific and technical knowledge.[36] In Price's world, politicians play a relatively minor role. Not only do they walk softly, carrying little sticks—they speak softly. Price sums up the demise of politics ever so well when he states that contemporary politicans speak not as "diligent representatives," jealous of their constituency's rights, but as "friendly bargainers," content to meet the common man's wants. And what does the common man want? He wants, says Price, to be left alone, "provided, of course, that technology can supply him with tranquilizers and television, the contemporary version of bread and circuses."[37] Thus, the Pricean world, in addition to four estates, comes to have two classes: the franchised and the disenfranchised. A person may speak the authoritative language of a decision maker only if he or she possesses the credentials of the "expert." The person who lacks these credentials—and the average citizen and the home-grown politician do lack them—must remain silent when any decision is to be made lest his or her "old-fashioned ways" stand in the way of progress. Politics is make-believe; technics is for real.

Science as It Is Threatened by Politics

To the degree that some critics worry that science is robbing politics of its authority, others like Joel Primack and Frank von Hippel fear that politics is debasing science. By politics, Primack and von Hippel do not understand the process by which the people shape their collective destiny either by direct participation or through representation. Rather, by politics, they understand power politics: the right of the powerful few to pursue their own ends at the expense of the powerless many. Primack and von Hippel are especially exercised by the executive branch's apparent interest in consolidating its own power both against that of the judicial branch, which strives to transcend partisan politics, and against that of the legislative branch, which attempts to respond to the people's wants and needs. Supposedly, when it is not bribing, manipulating, or intimidating spineless experts to do its bidding, the executive branch is suppressing, repressing, distorting, or at least misquoting the words of any expert who has a leg to stand on. As Primack and von Hippel see it, the only group that can break the executive branch's monopoly on and abuse of scientific knowledge is a circle of "outside" experts free to evaluate, criticize, and challenge the recommendations of "inside" experts.

In their *Advice and Dissent: Scientists in the Political Arena*, Primack and von Hippel point out that "outsiders" or public-interest scientists have already come to the aid of the people. They provide cases from the first Nixon administration, where scientific public-interest activities were able to counter executive irresponsibility, including not only serious potential damage from the SST, from nerve-gas storage/transport, and from accidental ABM warhead detonation, but also serious actual damage from the U.S. defoliation program in Vietnam.[38] So enthusiastic are Primack and von Hippel about public-interest science that they simply assume that the more *democratic* scientific advice is—that is, the more it corresponds to the public interest—the more "correct" it is, and vice versa. But who is it that determines when a bit of scientific advice is in the public's best interest and therefore "correct"? Presumably the public. But can a plurality of contending partisan groups first transform themselves into a national collectivity and then decide which of two or more scientific assertions is in its best interests? Were this Plato's *Republic*, it might make sense to speak of a public interest that transcends the interests of separate individuals; or were this Mill's Democracy, we could expect the truth first to emerge from the conflict of contending scientific opinions and then to be embraced by one and all. But this is neither Plato's nor Mill's world. It is twentieth-century America. Special interest groups rarely coalesce, and even when they do coalesce, they often fail to recognize the truth. In this connection, we may want to reflect upon cases in which the public sided either with the less scientifically correct position or, worse, with the scientifically incorrect position. The recombinant DNA controversy is a case in point.

Despite the fact that DNA experiments offer exciting and interesting potential both for advancing knowledge of fundamental biological processes and for the alleviation of human health problems, and despite the fact that molecular biologists themselves have demonstrated a remarkable willingness to impose controls on their genetic research, the public has frequently been more swayed by the media's sensationalist and biased view of genetic engineering than by the scientific community's sober and balanced account of this biotechnical advance. One of my colleagues, a biologist, reported the following incident to a group of academics assembled to study "Expertise and the Politics of Risk":

> I remember standing in line in a supermarket in 1980 when the latest issue of *The National Inquirer* caught my eye. The headline was "Geneticists on Verge of Creating Plant People" and inside was a picture of a tree with a human face

and arms which were gas pump handles. The gas pumps had been replaced with these genetically engineered trees which could not only produce gasoline (the sap) but also pump and deliver it. A second picture showed a "killer" cactus in army boots, shooting poisonous seeds, suggesting a war-related use. While this is laughable, perhaps one older gentleman behind me in line, viewing the same tabloid, turned to his companion and wondered out loud where all this was leading.[39]

Given that the gentleman's reaction in the anecdote is far from atypical, and given that local communities across the nation have managed to block relatively risk-free genetic experimentation meant to benefit them, we may wonder whether the public is indeed the best judge of its own best interest.

Science and Politics Cooperating in a Technological Era

If self-interested experts and politicians sometimes abuse their knowledge and power by manipulating each other, and if citizens often fail to distinguish between science fact and science fiction, then, seemingly, we have little choice but to deliver ourselves to whomever cares enough and knows enough to act in our best interests. But trust in a benign coterie of enlightened experts and rulers is no substitute for self-governance—for achieving whatever expertise we need to achieve in order to decide our separate and collective destinies wisely. We praise as well-behaved, little boys and girls who trust Mommy and Daddy to provide them with whatever is good for them; but we castigate as apathetic, mature adults who mindlessly trust the powers that be to construct and control their environment. A prefabricated heaven may be beautiful, but the people who live in it may as well be dolls living in a dolls' house; mute puppets that are moved from position to position without knowing why or even asking why. If we are to shape our own destiny—to build our however imperfect earths or, God forbid, uninhabitable hells—then we must participate in our own governance. As things stand, however, we will not be able to rule ourselves, no matter how willing we are to do so, unless existing public decision-making institutions design new mechanisms to maximize public input.

American Experiments in Public Participation. To date, participatory reforms in America have been mostly intended to expand the information available to the public and to communicate information about public preferences to decision makers. To a lesser extent, American participatory reforms have also sought to open the administrative process and to allow public representatives to take an active part in the development of policies. Two of the acts that have been specifically legislated to increase the public's information base are the Administrative Procedures Act and the Freedom of Information Act. The former act requires all federal agencies to publish proposed regulations in the *Federal Register* and to solicit public comments, which are taken into account in drafting the final regulations. Unfortunately, most citizens have neither the initiative, the resources, nor the access to expertise necessary to secure, let alone utilize, the 60,000-page-per-year report.[40] In a like vein, the Freedom of Information Act, as we shall see in Chapter 7, has proven to be a relatively toothless tiger.

Nevertheless, despite their limitations, both of these acts have apparently inspired a rash of participatory experiments, some of which have been relatively successful. Lay persons are now routinely included on advisory boards, national commissions, and institutional review boards. For example, in 1975, 45 agencies employed over 1,250 advisory committees with over 22,000 members.[41] Unfortunately, such improvements in lay participation do not necessarily signal a victory for popular democracy, since those who serve on this nation's boards and commissions are generally members of organized interest groups rather than representatives of the public at large.

European Experiments in Public Participation. Several European nations have had considerably more success than the United States in devising mechanisms for broad-based public participation in policymaking. In her *Technological Decisions and Democracy*, Dorothy Nelkin traces the growth of public demands for participation in Sweden, the Netherlands, and Austria. In Sweden, for example, the Riksdag approved a government proposal to sponsor study circles in the field of energy. Study circles have a long history in Sweden. They date back to the end of the nineteenth century, when they were inaugurated as a means to develop political democracy. Over the years these circles have generally focused on nontechnical issues, but in 1974 Sweden recognized that technical issues were also amenable to "ideological" discussion. The Ministries of Education and Industry paid around $650,000 to have seven large organizations (including labor unions, political parties, temperance movements, and church groups) educate approximately 80,000 Swedes about energy issues. Typically, the study circles covered questions such as the high energy demand in the Western world, the comparative economic costs and benefits of different energy sources, and the political and ethical problems posed by a reliance on nuclear energy as opposed to coal, oil, or gas.[42] After each study circle met for at least 10 hours, the organizations that had sponsored them released their results to each other and to the public at large. Although the study circles did not trigger any mass conversions toward or away from, say, a pronuclear policy, everyone who participated in the discussions apparently gained insight into the complexity of the issues. As a result of increased public understanding and feedback, the government eventually advanced a much more cautious nuclear policy than it would have advanced otherwise.[43]

Faced with similar questions about nuclear policy, Austrian officials organized a public information campaign. As part of this campaign, teams of experts—equally divided between supporters and opponents of nuclear energy—were asked first to prepare information on each of 10 themes (social and economic questions, cost effectiveness, general problems of energy policy, specific problems unique to Austria, risk assessment and evaluation, safety and security, control of nuclear power, hazardous waste disposal, cooling mechanisms, and biomedical questions) and then to distinguish between the technical (factual) and political (evaluative) arguments the themes evoked. Having done this, these experts debated each other on television primarily with reference to technical issues. The public was encouraged to submit questions for the experts, and during the course of the debates, the experts did in fact address many of the questions submitted.

Although Austria's information campaign was relatively successful in that the average citizen's knowledge about nuclear energy increased significantly, critics maintained that all the experts, including the "antinuclear" experts, were at rock bottom pronuclear, since most Austrian scientists are linked either to *government* research or to *industrial* applications in the field. Significantly, the self-confessed pronuclear government conceded that although the critics had a valid point, there was not much that could be done about the situation short of importing foreign scientists. In response to another criticism, namely, that the public was incapable of following the nuances of the debate to which they were privy, the government issued to all interested Austrians a free dictionary defining all the technical and economic terms used in the debates at a level that corresponded to the literacy of high school graduates. The Austrian government was not so successful in answering yet another objection, however, an objection that plagues most campaigns to increase citizen participation: namely, that it is Parliament, Congress, or some elected group of representatives that ultimately makes the decisions, and not the people in some sort of direct referendum, for example.[44]

Dorothy Nelkin's Program for Public Participation. The problem of representative versus participatory democracy is, of course, a crucial one that needs to be examined here, but not before we summarize Nelkin's general findings. Having studied numerous European experiments in public participation, Nelkin concludes that:

> (1) *Democratization requires participation at an early stage of the policy process*; (2) regardless of their technical nature, *political conflict and ambiguity are basic realities of technological decisions*; (3) if political participation is to be effective, *there must be means to improve public understanding of science*; (4) *participatory efforts are faced with difficult problems of defining "legitimate" interests*; and (5) *the forms of participation will vary according to the values that a society wishes to maximize.*[45]

What is particularly significant about Nelkin's conclusions is that, as she presents them, they offer guidance not only to policy experts but also to policymakers.

1. Democratization Requires Participation at an Early Stage of the Policy Process. Rather than first inaugurating a public policy and then educating the public toward "rubber-stamping" it, policymakers should consult the people "in the formation of initial policy intentions and objectives on the assumption that this is necessary if technology is to really reflect social priorities."[46] Such before-the-fact consultations are particularly useful for policy analysts. Unless policy analysts are aware of the people's value hierarchy, they will probably fail to include or to weigh accurately those costs, benefits, and risks that the people themselves perceive as germane to a given policy decision.

2. Political Conflict and Moral Ambiguity Are Basic Realities of Technological Decisions. This is so regardless of their technical nature. There is no better example of this truism than the abortion debate. Better information about what an abortion is, about how a fetus develops, and about which women have abortions has not brought the pro-choice and pro-life forces measurably closer. Similarly, better information about which nation has how much in its nuclear stockpile in no way resolves the question of either the prudence or the morality of this country's adding to its deadly heap. To insist that such questions are mainly technical is to cause ordinary citizens to withdraw from the fray, convinced that the political and ethical quandaries that used to occupy citizens' attention have been dissolved by the acid of technique.

3. There Must Be Means to Improve Public Understanding of Science. This is necessary if political participation is to be effective. Unless we want to give up on democracy and create a two-class structure divided along the lines of "smartness" and "dumbness," then concrete means must be devised to educate people not only during their school years but thereafter. Radio and television, for example, could be put to better use than they are now. Cable television already permits us to view debates in the House of Representatives as well as debates among local officials, and there is no reason why the Public Broadcasting System or the major commercial networks could not package technical information in an interesting and comprehensible fashion for citizens. Although widespread two-way communication vis television appears to be distant, it does offer possibilities both for educating citizens and for gauging public opinion. Such a potential is risky, however, because "program slant" would be critical to a vote taken immediately after a citizen had viewed a presentation. Careful monitoring would be necessary to present balanced presentation, but it is not clear what agent, if any, could be trusted to enforce fair play in the media.

4. Participatory Efforts Are Faced with Difficult Problems of Defining "Legitimate" Interests. Assume, for example, that the federal government wishes to site a nuclear power plant in a small New England town. Should this be a national, regional, or municipal issue? Does it make a difference if the people who are going to receive the benefit of cheaper electricity live not where the plant is located, but in the Midwest? Is the Midwesterner's interest in inexpensive energy more or less legitimate than the New Englander's interest in a risk-free environment? Should those who bear the risks of living near a projected nuclear plant refuse to accept those risks unless they will be the ones to receive any benefits that the plant produces?

5. The Forms of Participation A Society Fosters Will Vary According to the Values It Wishes to Maximize. Because our society values the "benefit" of efficiency, it sometimes views increased citizen participation as a cost. We know, for example, that a department chairperson who lets each of her colleagues speak his or her own mind at the weekly meeting will probably be criticized for not getting her reports in on time. Group decision making tends to proceed very slowly, especially if the decision makers are not pressed for time. On occasion, however, a decision has to be made quickly. During war, for example, military leaders have no time to consult their troops about what target they should attack when. Significantly, the public is generally willing to accept centralized authority under such stressful conditions. In the same way that siblings stop bickering when they sense that Mom and Dad really need their cooperation, soldiers know when to keep quiet and citizens know when to hold their peace. But even if efficiency ought to override participation in times of peril, it is not clear when or even if efficiency ought to override participation in nonperilous times. On the one hand, too little discussion makes it possible for forceful elites to ram their preferences down the throats of the masses. On the other hand, too much discussion grinds the policymaking process to a halt. If Aristotle's mean between extremes ever needed to be struck, it needs to be struck between those who want only the best and the brightest to speak as sparingly as possible and those who want everyone to discuss everything all the time. Quoting an Austrian civil servant, Dorothy Nelkin reminds us that "we know from history that an elitist system leads to political catastrophe. Real democracy, wide public participation, can certainly prevent such disasters through the same instinct of people."[47] What we do not know from history, however, is whether participatory democracy is possible in populous, heterogeneous, and complex societies. If it is not possible, then representative democracy, with all its attendant difficulties, is the best we can hope for.

THE DEMORALIZATION
OF CITIZENS BY EXPERTS

According to a number of political theorists, representative democracy may be workable when the people are represented by policymakers who have been elected by them, but it is not workable when the people are represented by policy experts whom they have not elected and who are not directly responsible to them. Articulating what is the minority position, Joel Primack and Frank von Hippel argue that, contrary to common misconceptions, experts who contribute to the policymaking process are indeed the representatives of the people in the sense that they are obligated "to provide their fellow citizens with the information and analyses necessary for effective participation in the political process."[48] Supposedly, experts are burdened with this obligation simply because they are at times privy to information without which the people cannot intelligently rule themselves and because they, like all government employees, are bound by that code of ethics which teaches policymakers and policy experts alike to "put loyalty to the highest moral principles and to country above loyalty to persons, party, or Government department."[49] Primack and von Hippel seem to carry the notion of representation further, however. At times they speak as if the people should have their own set of experts ready to do battle with the experts at the service of the government, especially the executive branch of the federal government. They claim that the former experts serve the public interest, whereas the latter experts, succumbing to the pressures of status and salary, serve not the public interest but those of big government or of big business or of the military. What Primack and von Hippel fail to analyze adequately, however, is the notion of the public interest. Can experts speak for the public interest; can they stand outside the multiplicity of particular partisan notions of the public good and announce what is really in the best interest of one and all? Or are experts just as likely to mistake *their version of* the public interest for *the* public interest, as anyone else would do?

Considerations such as these prompt some critics to favor scenarios in which each special interest group has its own set of experts who view themselves as that group's advocates. The problem with this adversarial model is that it encourages experts to package the facts in ways that will support the group's claims even if the unadulterated facts tend to defeat those claims. Moreover, the adversarial model also requires a supposedly qualified public to decide which group's version of the truth is the truth. Are Ralph Nader's experts painting a portrait of unnecessary gloom and doom when they say that the American people are slowly being poisoned to death by means of pesticides, food additives, and pollutants? Or are the government's experts looking through rose-colored glasses when they proclaim that the American people have never been healthier? Only a public sufficiently well-versed in the pros and cons of a policy problem has any hope of identifying its real friends and foes.

Mechanisms for Improving
and Publicizing Expert Opinion

In order to avoid, or at least to minimize, abuses of what may be a promising solution to the problem of the concentration of knowledge in the hands of the few, some theorists have pressed for the establishment of science courts as a means of adjudicating disputes among experts. The science court begins with the assumption that questions of scientific or technical fact can be separated from questions of values, and that scientists are experts only when it comes to questions of fact. The science court continues with the conviction that disagreement about technical facts can be clarified, if not also resolved, provided that "case managers" are selected to defend each side of a controversial issue. Case managers would first defend with documentation the scientific or technical facts grounding their respective cases. They then would exchange notes, examining each other's claims and identifying points of agreement and disagreement. If agreement were reached, the dispute would be resolved. If agreement were not reached, a hearing, open to the public and governed by "distinguished referees," would be held. The referees would confine the discussion to "the facts," and a panel of disinterested, "sophisticated scientific judges" would, after the hearing, decide if one or more of the adversaries were wrong, if their differences were legitimate, and/or if more investigation or analysis were needed.[50]

Allan Mazor, a staunch supporter of the science court, admits that as promising as the idea of the science court seems, it is not unassailable. One objection is that facts and values are inseparable in considering public policy issues, and the more controversial the issue, the greater the uncertainty over the facts. To this objection Mazor answers that although a science court cannot promise to deliver *the truth*, it can "approximate the truth" better than other arrangements, such as disparagement, peer review, mediation, expert committees, and traditional hearings.[51] Similarly, although a science court cannot always separate facts from values, it can easily separate factual questions such as "How many cancers per year will be produced in a population exposed to radiation?" from normative questions such as "How many cancers per year should be accepted in exchange for inexpensive electricity generated by a radiation-emitting nuclear power plant?"[52] A related type of objection, for which Mazor has no real reply, is the criticism that mechanisms such as a science court can obscure the political and social dimensions of a debate. Barry M. Casper and Paul David Wellstone provide a case in point. Governor Rudy Perpich of Minnesota urged that a science court be convened to adjudicate a dispute between several electric power cooperatives that were building a high-voltage transmission line straight across Minnesota farm land and the militant protecting farmers whose land was thereby violated. After much discussion, Perpich got the co-ops to agree to a science court provided that only issues of health and safety would be debated. Interestingly, the farmers scoffed at this deal. For the farmers, the high-voltage transmission constituted not so much a potential injury as an actual insult to their autonomy. Indeed, what bothered the farmers most was the fact that the co-ops had been granted rights of eminent domain to some of their land. Thus, what the farmers wished to debate was not the scientific and technical issues concerned with health and safety, but the social and political issues associated with questions of "need, alternative routes, eminent domain, and the impact of the line on an agricultural environment."[53]

Casper and Wellstone's analysis of this case reminds us that it is a political issue whether or not to convene a science court. The farmers didn't want the kind of science court Governor Perpich had in mind. They didn't want "disinterested, sophisticated scientific judges" deciding whether or not high-voltage transmission lines constitute a health and/or safety risk. What the farmers wanted was an adversary hearing with elected public officials deciding whether or not profit-making co-ops are entitled to as much eminent domain as the Minnesota Environmental Quality Board, to name just one agency, had granted them. Casper and Wellstone's analysis also reminds us that even when a science court is appropriate, self-interested parties might try to set the agenda to promote their own ends. Indeed, whatever body controls the agenda for the science court, that body will have the power to decide what counts as an important issue. If government agencies set the agenda of the science court, then the government will be able to extend its control over expertise. If the experts themselves set the court's agenda, then they may be tempted to debate only interesting (read: highly technical) issues, despite the fact that the public is not the least concerned about such arcane debates. Thus, it would seem that the people themselves should determine not only whether a science court is an appropriate response to a given situation, but also what its agenda should be if it is convened.

A final criticism leveled against the science court is that even if the people control the science court's agenda, and even if the experts in charge of the court as well as those testifying before it discharge their duties to the people both responsibly and responsively, it is not clear whether policymakers would in any way bind themselves by the court's determinations. Mazor, for example, is enough of a realist to admit that policymakers use or ignore scientific facts and analyses "depending on whether or not they are consistent with their prior goals."[54] Nevertheless, he insists that there are limits on policymakers' wheelings and dealings:

> Opponents of the fluoridation of drinking water, or of legalizing smoking or sale of marijuana, might well maintain their objections even if there were overwhelming evidence that these substances were not toxic. But I doubt that proponents of fluoridation and the legalization of marijuana could maintain their positions effectively in the face of clear evidence that these substances were highly toxic.[55]

Although the science court has its problems, clearly it could be modified in ways that would enhance democratic decision making. One suggestion is to preserve the adversarial "case manager" component of the court and to dispense with the "scientific judge" component. Among others, Casper questions the need for scientific judges, noting that this assumes that politicians and other citizens are unable to weigh the claims of experts and judge for themselves.[56] But if yesterday's beleagured housewives, for example, could figure out which of 100 detergents to purchase, then today's career women can decide, after hearing evidence on both sides of the cyclamates coin, whether or not artificially sweetened products pose a threat to their health.

Mechanisms for Improving and Publicizing Public Opinion

Throughout this whole discussion we have been proceeding on the assumption that no matter how complicated it has become, the policymaking process remains hospitable to citizen participation. According to John Byrne, however, this assumption is simply unwarranted. Comments Byrne:

> The world of cost-benefit analysis has no need of a participative citizenry. The processes of public decision-making depend in this world upon the identification of objective values. It is only with their identification that rational solutions can be found. To involve the citizenry in the process of identifying values could only result in contamination of the process, for all they can offer are subjective assessments of their idiosyncratic circumstances. To operate effectively, the world of cost-benefit analysis must be insulated from and preemptive of the participation of its citizens.[57]

If Byrne is correct, then all that is left of the idea of citizen is a "glorified notion of consumer."[58] That is to say, in a world ruled by policy experts, governance is a "consumptive good:"[59]

Citizens decide whether and to what degree they are satisfied with the products of governance but they have no responsibility for the production of governance or even overseeing its production. Indeed, the expectation is that citizens have no substantial interest in such matters.[66]

That Byrne is not altogether off the mark seems clear. The notion of the citizen-consumer is so pervasive that college students view course selection time as a pilgrimage through the marketplace. More than one student has told me that she shops around for her courses, that she wants the best product for her money, and that the teachers have to package their information and peddle their ideas if they wish to maintain healthy enrollments. This is a disturbing commentary on contemporary psychology, one that forces us to consider the possibility that experts are "demoralizing" the populace in two ways. First, they contribute to the typical citizen's sense of ignorance and powerlessness; as a result, the citizen becomes either alienated (aggressive) or apathetic (passive). Second, a very visible and vocal community of experts can easily erode the typical citizen's desire to make decisions. It is relatively easy for the citizen, especially the materially satisfied citizen, to let those "in the know" make crucial decisions for him/her.

In *Speaking Truth to Power*, Aaron Wildavsky ponders the problem of the apathetic citizen and argues that it is the primary task of policy analysts to make themselves dispensable. That is, policy analysts should take it upon themselves to devise ways that will first stimulate and then facilitate citizen participation in the policymaking process. According to Wildavsky, typical citizens have neither the desire nor the time to involve themselves in the resolution of every matter of public policy.[61] In order to be experts on nuclear contamination, the antiballistic missile, cyclamates, the artificial heart, and seat-belt safety, we would have to read all the relevant material and attend all the relevant meetings. There would be little time left in the day to attend to our professional and personal duties. Certainly there would be no time for fun. Nevertheless, each of us will be touched by at least some issues from time to time. When this happens, we should become "amateur experts" on our respective pet issue, gleaning information from professional experts willing and able to explain the nuances of the targeted issue. For example, policy analysts should explain their calculations to those populations that will be positively or negatively affected by them, encouraging their audience to discuss those normative questions that are not the analysts' to resolve. Had the Minnesota farmers had their way, they would have had not a science court, but the kind of people's court this format would tend to produce.

Admittedly, any such forum would be time-consuming and costly. But if such forums were conducted on the local level, and if policy advisers, policy analysts, and subject-area specialists volunteered their services on a fairly routine basis, perhaps they could work. On occasion, such forums will prove a luxury. For example, as we noted above, some policy decisions have to made quickly. This is not to suggest, however, as some argue, that most policy decisions have to be made quickly and that the only viable form of public participation is the push-button referendum. Equip each television with a voting channel, and let the citizens register their preferences between the hours of 6 and 8 P.M. Unfortunately, "instant democracy" has the same disadvantages that instant mashed potatoes and instant pudding have. In the same way that instant food is a poor substitute for "real" food, instant democracy is a poor substitute for that type of democracy that is created through sustained discussions. To be sure, instant pudding is better than no pudding at all, and instant democracy is better than no democracy at all; but in the same way that a steady diet of instant food can cause a person to lose all interest in food, a steady diet of anonymous pollings and votings can cause a citizen to lose the taste not only for politics but also for ethics.

In a democratic, pluralistic society, ethics progresses by means of conversation and by means of a mutual search for the human good. To exclude the citizenry from policy discussions is not only to subvert the democratic process, but to erode moral dialogue. Thus, whatever else policy experts may do, they should devise mechanisms that will enhance citizen participation. The less necessary and mystifying policy experts make themselves, the more they will have succeeded. The moral trap of the professional, as Max Weber knew, is "living off" instead of "living for" the troubles of their clients. Doing oneself out of a job is the best way for the policy expert to do analysis, to give advice, and to share specialized knowledge not only with high-level policymakers but with ordinary citizens.

NOTES

1. Marshall Berman, "Modernity–Yesterday, Today, and Tomorrow," *Berkshire Review: Modernization and Its Discontents* (1981), 8.

2. George A. Kelly, "The Expert as Historical Actor," *Daedelus* 92, no. 3 (Summer 1963), 533.

3. Thomas Kuhn, *The Structure of Scientific Revolutions* (Chicago: University of Chicago Press, 1962), 113.

4. Richard R. Nelson, *The Moon and the Ghetto: An Essay on Public Policy Analysis* (New York: W. W. Norton & Company, Inc., 1977), 13.

5. Ibid., 31.

6. Ida R. Hoos, *Systems Analysis in Public Policy: A Critique* (Berkeley: University of California Press, 1972), 159.

7. Ibid.

8. Nelson, *The Moon and the Ghetto*, 31–32.

9. Arnold Meltsner, *Policy Analysts in the Bureaucracy* (Berkeley: University of California Press, 1976), 80.

10. Ibid., 50.

11. Ibid.

12. Herbert Goldhamer, *The Adviser* (New York: Elsevier Publishing Co., Inc., 1978), 15.

13. Ibid., 130–131.

14. Robert E. Lane, "The Decline of Politics and Ideology in a Knowledgeable Society," *American Sociological Review* 31, no. 5 (October 1966), 650.

15. Ibid., 652–53.

16. Ibid., 653.

17. Robert N. Bellah, "Social Science as Practical Reason," in *Ethics, The Social Sciences and Policy Analysis*, eds. Daniel Callahan and Bruce Jennings (New York: Plenum Press, 1983), 55.

18. Michael Walzer, "Political Action: The Problem of Dirty Hands," in *War and Moral Responsibility*, eds. Marshall Cohen, Thomas Nagel, and Thomas Scanlon (Princeton, N.J.: Princeton University Press, 1979), 63.

19. Niccolò Machiavelli, *The Prince* (New York: Modern Library edition, 1950), 57.

20. Max Weber, "Politics as a Vocation," in *From Max Weber: Essays in Sociology*, trans. and eds. Hans H. Gerth and C. Wright Mills (New York: Oxford University Press, 1946), 125-26.

21. Ibid.

22. Carl Schmitt, *The Concept of the Political*, trans., intro., and notes by George Schwab (New Brunswick, N.J.: Rutgers University Press, 1976).

23. Thomas Hobbes, *Leviathan*, (New York: Collier Books edition, 1962), 237.

24. Ibid.

25. B. F. Skinner, *Beyond Freedom and Dignity* (New York: A Bantam/Vintage Books, 1972), 204.

26. Ibid., 204-205.

27. John McDermott, "Technology: The Opiate of the Intellectuals," in *Technology as a Social and Political Phenomenon* (New York: John Wiley & Sons, 1976), 92.

28. Edward C. Banfield, "Policy Science as Metaphysical Madness," in *Bureacrats, Policy Analysts, Statesmen: Who Leads?* (Washington, D.C.: American Enterprise Institute for Public Policy Research, 1980), 1-19.

29. Theodore Roszak, *Where the Wasteland Ends: Politics and Transcendence in Post-industrial Society* (Garden City: Doubleday and Co., Inc., 1972), 53.

30. Albert Wohlstetter, "Strategy and the Natural Scientists," in *Scientists and National Policy-Making*, eds. Robert Gilpin and Christopher Wrights (New York: Columbia University Press, 1964), 191.

31. Ian D. Clark, "Expert Advice in the Controversy About Supersonic Transport in the United States," *Minerva* 13, no. 4 (October 1974), 419.

32. Ibid., 430.

33. Daniel Guttman and Barry Wilner, *The Shadow Government: The Government's Multi-Billion Dollar Giveaway of Its Decision-Making Powers to Private Management Consultants, "Experts," and Think Tanks* (New York: Pantheon, 1976).

34. Langdon Winner, *Autonomous Technology* (Cambridge, Mass.: The MIT Press, 1977), 146.

35. Ibid., 147.

36. Don K. Price, *The Scientific Estate* (Cambridge: Harvard University Press, 1967), 133-134.

37. Ibid., p. 143.

38. Joel Primack and Frank von Hippel, *Advice and Dissent: Scientists in the Political Arena* (New York: Basic Books, Inc., Publ. 1974), 128-238.

39. Barton E. Slatko, "Comments on Rouse—Recombinant DNA: Reflections on Scientific Knowledge and Its Place in Public Controversy," in "Expertise and the Politics of Risk," *Berkshire Review* 18, (1983), 48.

40. Dorothy Nelkin, "Science and Technology Policy and the Democratic Process," in *Five Year Outlook* 12 (Washington, D.C.: National Science Foundation, 1980), 487.

41. Ibid., 488.

42. Dorothy Nelkin, *Technological Decisions and Democracy* (Beverly Hills: Sage Publications, 1977), 61-62. Copyright © 1977 by Sage Publications, Inc. Reprinted by permission of Sage Publications, Inc.

43. Ibid., 63-64.

44. Ibid., 80-82.

45. Ibid., 95-99.

46. Ibid., 95.

47. Ibid., 98-99.

48. Primack and von Hippel, *Advice and Dissent*, 108.

49. Ibid.

50. Task Force of the Presidential Advisory Group on Anticipated Advances in Science and Technology, "The Science Court Experiment: An Interim Report," *Science* 193 (1976), 653-56.

51. Allan Mazor, "Science Courts," *Minerva* 15, no. 1 (Spring 1977), 2-4.

52. Ibid., 10.

53. Barry M. Casper and Paul David Wellstone, "The Science Court on Trial in Minnesota," *Hastings Center Report* 8, no. 4 (August 1978), 7.

54. Mazor, "Science Courts," 14.

55. Ibid.

56. Casper, "Technology, Policy and Democracy: Is the Proposed Science Court What We Need?", 31.

57. John Byrne, "A Critique of Beauchamp and Braybrooke-Schotch," in *Ethical Issues in Government*, ed. Norman E. Bowie (Philadelphia: Temple University Press, 1981), 204-205.

58. Ibid., 205.

59. Ibid.

60. Ibid.

61. Aaron Wildavsky, *Speaking Truth to Power: The Art and Craft of Policy Analysis* (Boston: Little Brown and Company, 1979), 252-77.

Chapter 4

Dirty Hands, Many Hands, No Hands:
The Policy Expert Within
the Bowels of the Bureaucracy

Although the policy expert's ethical dilemmas are not the same as those of the policymaker, nevertheless, it is helpful to understand the ways in which the policymaker's moral quandaries are both similar to and different from those of the policy expert. In recent years, many political philosophers have been preoccupied with the classic problem of "dirty hands," the possibility that public life may require officials to act in ways that would be wrong in private life. This problem appears in a variety of ways in the philosophical literature. For example, in *The Prince*, written in the sixteenth century, Machiavelli argues that a monarch cannot afford to be a sheep among wolves. Like those who would devour him, the prince must learn how not to be good and how to use this knowledge according to the necessity of the case. In particular, Machiavelli advises the price to redefine the terms *virtue* and *vice*. A vice is that which, if followed, would lead to the state's ruin; a virtue is that which, if followed, would lead to the state's greater security and well-being. So, for example, a price must be cruel rather than merciful, feared rather than loved, because

> Men worry less about doing an injury to one who makes himself loved then to one who makes himself feared. The bond of love is one which men, wretched creatures that they are, break when it is to their advantage to do so; but fear is strengthened by a dread of punishment which is always effective.[1]

Moreover, a prince must be ready to break promises—to be a fox, not a patsy. He must be the great feigner and pretender—a rogue in an altar boy's attire, who will be praised by one and all so long as he maintains a prosperous state.

Although some of us may be repelled by the prince, it is hard to trivialize the benefits he provides: a flourishing economy, military might, law and order. His hands may be dirty, but the citizens' bellies are full. So perhaps the prince's political prowess excuses his "pecadillos"; and perhaps, just perhaps, the public realm is ruled by an ethical system that permits or even requires what is forbidden by the ethical system governing the private realm.

Significantly, writing 350 years after Machiavelli, Max Weber defends a version of the two-moralities viewpoint. As Weber sees it, the political realm is characterized by power, or what he sometimes terms "force" or "legitimate violence." Not only do governments send young men to war and criminals to execution, they collect taxes, compel children to be schooled, and control the flow of traffic. Given that politicians live, move, and have their being in a world dominated by power, coercion, violence, and force, what kind of ethical standards rule their professional activities? It is here that Weber introduces a distinction between an ethic of responsibility and an ethic of ultimate ends. The former asks about the "foreseeable results of one's action," while the latter asks only about the purity of intentions—"The Christian does rightly and leaves the results with the Lord." Weber's objection to the application of the ethic of ultimate ends in the public arena is that given the irrationality of human history, the complexity of human psychology, and the enormouse effort it takes to keep the human enterprise afloat, the ethics of ultimate ends is a luxury the human race cannot afford. Pure intentions are not enough when the human species' survival is at risk, and those who are steering the ship of state must be willing at times "to pay the price of using morally dubious means or at least dangerous ones" if they are to save the lives of those who depend upon them.[2] Nevertheless, if the politician rejects the ethic of ultimate ends in favor of an ethic of responsibility, he or she is not likely to be praised any more than the politician who follows his or her conscience no matter what the consequences. Any politician who has been around long enough knows the meaning of the phrase "Damned if you do, damned if you don't." On the one hand, if the President, for example, refuses to consider the development of new nuclear weapons despite the fact that aggressor nations are doing so, then the public will probably fault him for indulging his pacifist, moral point of view at the risk of imperiling one and all. On the other hand, if the President fails to follow the ethic of ultimate ends—that is, the imperatives of his personal conscience—his family and friends may chide him. "How can you support the development of new nuclear weapons, Daddy? Before you were elected, you told us that you were morally opposed to any such development."

THE PROBLEM OF DIRTY HANDS

Walzer's Defense

Sympathizing with the politician's plight, Michael Walzer describes the politician's dilemma as follows:

> [A] particular act of government (in a political party or in the state) may be exactly the right thing to do in utilitarian terms and yet leave the man who does it guilty of a moral wrong. The innocent man, afterwards, is no longer innocent. If on the other hand he remains innocent, chooses, that is, the "ab-

solutist" side . . . , he not only fails to do the right thing (in utilitarian terms), he may also fail to measure up to the duties of his office (which imposes on him a considerable responsibility for consequences and outcomes).[3]

Walzer provides two cases that exemplify this dilemma: (1) In order to win an election, politician X must make a deal with a dishonest ward boss, involving a shady financial transaction. Convinced that his opponent, a totally incompetent moral nerd, will win the election unless he placates the ward boss, politician X gives in and negotiates the deal. (2) In order to find out where a terrorist has hidden a bomb that will probably kill and maim scores of people, politician Y, known as a defender of human rights, orders the terrorist tortured, convinced that he must do so for the sake of the people who might otherwise die in the explosions.[4]

According to Walzer, both of these men have done the right thing in the sense that both of them have acted so as to produce the greatest ratio of good to evil for everyone. Nevertheless, both of these men are likely to feel guilty, for in another sense of the term "wrong" they have also both done wrong by violating their duties ("Don't cheat" and "Don't inflict pain"), as specified by the Ten Commandments, for example. Moreover, those among us who would have condemned these two men had they not performed the utility-maximizing action are probably the same people who are condemning them now for not adhering to the Ten Commandments. The most direct way out of this cul de sac would be to bite the bullet and exclaim: "Utilitarianism is *the* moral point of view. Not only politicians but everyone at all times and in all places should abide by the Principle of Utility." But Walzer refuses to take the easy way out. Rather, he argues that even if we cannot *justify* the actions of politicians X and Y ("They performed the right actions"), we ought either to *excuse* X and Y ("Although they performed the wrong actions, extenuating circumstances were such that their culpability is somewhat less than it might have otherwise been") or at least to *forgive* X and Y ("Although they are without either justification or excuse for their wrong actions, let us nonetheless reassimilate our erring politicians back into our fold because 'them' could very easily have been 'us' "). We should, however, be sparing with such excuses and forgivenesses, meting them out only to those persons who not only feel regret for their wrong actions but also are willing to accept responsibility—and even punishment—for them.

Walzer develops this point by contrasting the respective states of mind of Machiavelli's prince, Max Weber's political bureaucrat, and Camus's just assassins. It is difficult for most people to trust Machiavelli's prince, since he is too matter-of-fact about his moral transgressions. He wields his power in ways that are bound to sicken those who have been treated as mere means in the march toward politically expedient ends. So, too, Weber's political bureaucrat is not likely to inspire trust among the masses. Anyone who is willing to sell his soul to the devil in order to serve the people is suspect. In the background looms the spectre of Faust, who sold his soul not to benefit mankind but to profit himself. In contrast to the Machiavellian prince and Weberian bureaucrat, notes Walzer, Camus's assassins provide welcome relief. Because they are willing to die for their acts of destruction, Camus insists that a group of assassins are, in the strictest sense of the term, "justified." The assassins' willingness to accept all the consequences of their actions renders those actions right.[5]

Although Walzer wonders whether it is every really right to assassinate someone, he also doubts whether it is always really wrong to do so. Certainly, he believes that it is within the limits of moral reason either to excuse or to forgive a group of assassins, even if their actions cannot finally be justified. No doubt even the absolutists among us would find some kind words for the assassins of a cruel tyrant who kills children for sport. And were these assassins to confess publicly their "crime," and to go to their death gladly for it, our kind words for them would probably multiply. Admittedly, points out Walzer, neither the situation of the politician who negotiates the shady deal nor that of the politician who orders the terrorist's torture is strictly analogous to that of a group of just assassins. Whereas instruments of punishment exist for those who break legal rules for moral reasons, there are no comparable instruments of punishment for those who break moral rules for political reasons. If such instruments of punishment were available, says Walzer, "Dirty hands would be no problem. We would simply honor the man who did bad in order to do good, and at the same time we would punish him."[6] Nevertheless, even though Walzer's politicians escape the criminal's fate of incarceration or even death, they do not escape the sinner's fate. As Walzer constructs the cases, the politician up for election is "reluctant even to consider the deal," questions his true motives, has serious scruples about cutting a little moral corner here and there, and feels lousy about making the deal. Similarly, the politician who orders the torture continues to believe "that torture is wrong, indeed abominable, not just sometimes, but always."[7] Somehow the knowledge that a politician suffers pangs of conscience reassures us. Indeed, even the bare belief that a politician is the type of person who would do private penance for politically expedient but morally unjustifiable actions enables us to excuse and to forgive him or her—if not to justify and to forget his or her actions.

Goldman's Critique

In a challenging critique of Walzer, Alan H. Goldman argues that the same ethics governs all of us both in the public and in the private realm, and that ethics is best described as a set of rules that reflect an ordered hierarchy of rights. Should we accept Goldman's moral point of view, we will analyze Walzer's two examples quite differently than Walzer. Argues Goldman:

> A candidate may have to make a deal with an unscrupulous boss to fix a contract in order to get elected, if he is convinced that his opponent, if elected, will fail to honor rights more precious than economic rights to fair bidding. Otherwise he has no excuse. At the other extreme in circumstances, it is true that a terrorist without an urgent cause may have to be tortured to find out where bombs that will kill innocent people are hidden, but this is certainly not a case of mere utilities overriding rights. Appeal to national interest or security may be legitimate if the appeal is to rights of citizens that are genuinely threatened from without or within, otherwise not.[8]

The appeal of Goldman's analysis is twofold: (1) Like the utilitarian, he provides an overarching concept that fuses the moralities of the private and public realms. To the degree that the utilitarian appeals to the maximization of general utility (pleasure or happiness), to that same degree Goldman appeals to the notion of rights. As he sees it, rights—and not utility—reign supreme in both the public and the private realm. (2) Unlike Walzer—who, by the way, is no utilitarian—Goldman attempts to justify and not merely to excuse or to forgive the politician who must violate lesser rights in order to preserve greater rights. According to Goldman, such violations do not involve wrongdoing even though they may be occasion for profound regret and reparation.

Although Goldman's tidy solution to the paradox of dirty hands is promising, it is ultimately disappointing. Goldman suggests that the politician's duty to protect negative rights takes precedence over his/her duty to provide for positive rights, and that the politician's duty to protect individual rights, be they negative or positive, takes precedence over his/her duty to promote aggregate welfare by regulating the economy and providing public goods and services. In Goldman's world, negative rights are "rights not to be harmed, mistreated or denied respect"; positive rights are ".rights to have certain needs or interests satisfied by the actions of others"; and aggregate utility is some combination of "majority wants" or interests, not as vital as those interests we term "rights," but which nonetheless play a significant role in the so-called "good life."[9]

In the abstract, Goldman's is a compelling hierarchy. Most of us do put our rights not to be harmed ahead of our rights to be benefited; and most of us are ready to forsake group utility in order to protect, preserve, and foster each other's individual rights. Nevertheless, despite the intuitive appeal of Goldman's hierarchy, it cannot withstand the pressure of concerted questioning precisely because the moral realm is not tidy. It is, at best, very messy. Rights do not always trump utilities. Sometimes utilities trump rights—and it's "right" that they do so. Ordinarily, we may insist that a highly profitable pantyhose factory ought to be shut down if it seriously violates either workers' rights to occupational safety or local residents' rights to healthful air and water. But I doubt very much that we would persist in playing our ace of rights if we discovered that the production of some good vital to our economy, such as electricity, was somewhat hazardous both to workers and to the environment. My guess is that under such conditions utility would be allowed to reign supreme with only a few voices raised in protest. As David Luban has pointed out, Kafka may have had a moral right to have all his books burned upon his death, but that does not necessarily mean that his heirs would have done wrong by sparing *The Trial* from the fires. Comments Luban: "It is simply not clear that Kafka's right trumps the value to the world of great art."[10]

To this line of reasoning, Goldman replies that we are misunderstanding him. Whenever it seems morally appropriate for a utility to trump a right, as in our electricity example or in Luban's Kafka example, then that utility will turn out to be a right in disguise. Rights emerge from utilities much in the same way that butterflies emerge from their cocoons. When we speak, for example, about products without which the economy would fail we are no longer talking about "mere utilities," we are talking about rights to basic goods like food, clothing, heat, and shelter, and our rights to such necessities transcend our rights to occupational health and safety as well as to crystal clean air and water. What is problematic about Goldman's initially plausible retort, however, is that it fails to address those hard cases when the butterfly is still in the cocoon, but isn't quite ready to come out. We want to know, for example, how vital affordable electricity is for all of us before we declare it a right that trumps, for example, workers' rights to occupational health and safety. When I tell Joe that Massachusetts Electric cannot spend any more money on protecting him from job-related hazards without jacking up his electric bills so high that he cannot afford to pay them, I want Joe to say, "Heh! That's OK. The assurance of a well-lit and warm home is more important to me than protecting me from risks x, y, and z at work." I don't want Joe to say, "Heh! I'd rather have me as well as you spend yet more on electricity so that I can go to work in the morning knowing that I'll probably be back safe and sound for dinner in the evening." Although I would like to be reassured by Goldman that when utilities clout rights, the "clouting" utilities are really rights in disguise, I suspect that the moral realm is considerably less well-behaved than he assumes. I fear that every once in a while, a very real individual right must give way to group utility. Were this not the case, there would be no tragedy in our world, and, as far as I can tell, tragedy is always lurking behind our doors.

THE PROBLEM OF MANY HANDS

What is ultimately disappointing about both Walzer's and Goldman's analysis of the problem of dirty hands is that it oversimplifies the moral complexity of the policy process. Were we dealing only with the moral point of view of *a* prince, or *a* sacrificial lamb, or *an* assassin, then we could argue with this "solitary figure," showing him how his ethical paradigm does not jibe with that of ordinary folk. But, as Dennis F. Thompson rightly points out, policymaking is not the tale of a few great individuals "single-handedly gathering information and implementing decisions."[11] Rather it is the saga of a multiplicity of individuals, speaking a great variety of tongues and contributing their two cents' worth of wisdom to a staggering number of issues. The persons who initially formulate a problem are generally not the ones who ultimately resolve it; and quite often no one really knows how many people did or did not contribute to its solution. Thompson observes that difficult as the problem of dirty hands may be, it is not nearly so difficult as what he dubs the "problem of many hands." The problem of dirty hands surfaced in a simpler era when we knew whom to hold accountable and whom to blame for what. The problem of many hands emerges at a time when so many cooks are stirring the political pot that "it is difficult even in principle to identify who is morally responsible for political outcomes."[12]

Surely, the problem of many hands is one that faces policy experts routinely.

Unless experts are able both to recognize and to accept responsibility for their occupational decisions and actions, and unless we as well as they know who is morally responsible for what, this nation's ethical sensitivities are likely to be eroded in particularly destructive ways. Vietnam and Watergate are not so much the stories of evil individuals performing wrong actions as the tales of foiled and/or flaunted lines of responsibility. What is frightening about contemporary policymaking is the feeling that the decisions most likely to affect society for better or worse are made not by identifiable persons but by an amorphous collectivity whose willy-nilly processes cannot be stopped once they are started.

In an effort to overcome this pessimistic view of the policymaking process, Thompson argues that although it is sometimes difficult to ascribe moral responsibility to those who are involved in the making of public policy, it is far from impossible to do so. Unfortunately, standard attempts to make these difficult ascriptions—grounded, as they are, on notions of hierarchical and collective responsibility—often obscure rather than reveal the agents actually responsible for a policy decision. Therefore, Thompson urges us to apply the notion of personal responsibility—grounded on a combination of causal criteria, the concept of intention, and the idea of role—whenever we wish to get to the bottom (or the top) of things.

The Ascription of Moral Responsibility
to Policy Experts

The Hierarchical Model of Responsibility. Whatever its other merits or demerits, Thompson's theory is helpful when it comes to ascribing responsibility to policy experts. Insofar as policy experts are concerned, the hierarchical notion of responsibility is particularly problematic. According to this model, each agent in the policymaking process is responsible for a definite set of functions which he or she never oversteps. Those who are higher up in the bureaucracy supervise those who are lower down; and the lower one stands on the bureaucratic totem pole, the fewer significant decisions one makes. The people on the top, the elected policymakers, make the decisions; the people on the bottom, among whom are situated most policy experts, simply rubber-stamp and/or carry them out. Therefore, or so the argument goes, ultimate responsibility for policy decisions falls on the person who stands highest in the formal or informal chain of authority. Thompson points out that top policymakers usually feel obligated to acknowledge that the "buck stops here." For example, in private, President Kennedy castigated the CIA, the Joint Chiefs, and any underling who knew about the ill-fated Bay of Pigs invasion in advance. Nevertheless, in public, he accepted "sole responsibility" for the fiasco.[13] Similarly, Nixon assumed total responsibility for Watergate on the grounds that only a "cowardly" leader would pin the blame on the low man on the totem pole.[14] To be sure, this is a tidy way of ascribing responsibility. "Take me to your leader," cries the ethicist who is operating on the hierarchical model, "and I'll give you a scapegoat so that none of you lowly experts will have to pay for your sins. You will be absolved on the grounds that you were either following the orders of your superiors or adhering to the procedures of your organization."

Tidiness notwithstanding, the hierarchical model seems deficient in several respects. First, it is not clear that a contemporary bureaucracy resembles Plato's *Republic*, an ideal society in which each person is assigned that one function he or she can perform best and only that one function. Most bureaucracies are "blooming, buzzing confusions" in which it is usually not clear who is responsible for what task. Authority is routinely delegated as those at the top of the pyramid find it impossible to make all the decisions all of the time. So too is authority routinely usurped in many and subtle ways. For example, when an entire office of policy analysts is under pressure to complete a project as quickly as possible, those who are willing and able to work extra hours will influence the final contours of the project in ways that those who are unwilling or unable to go the extra mile will not. It matters not if the "eager beavers" have smaller offices, less wordy titles, and less official authority than their bosses who come to work around 9 A.M. and leave promptly at 5 P.M. If they work longer and harder than their bosses, the final report will probably reflect their point of view rather than their superiors'. Second, it is not clear that those at the top of the hierarchy should assume total responsibility for their underlings' decisions and actions. For a superior to take the blame, or more likely the praise, for his or her subordinates' thinkings and doings can be unfair both to the superior and to the subordinate. It can be unfair to the superior insofar as he or she was nonnegligently ignorant of his or her subordinates' decisions and actions; and it can be unfair to the subordinate insofar as the superior deprives him or her of a measure of disapprobation or approbation. In order to develop as moral agents, as persons who view ourselves as making things happen to ourselves and to others and therefore as accountable to self and to others, we need both positive and negative feedback. Thus, if other people take the credit or blame for our moral successes and failures, respectively, they retard our moral development.

The Collective Model of Responsibility. In an effort to overcome the defects of the hierarchical model, some theorists have forwarded a collective model for the ascription of responsibility. One version of the collective model holds that no individual is morally responsible for any of the collectivity's decisions and actions; rather, the collectivity as a whole is responsible. "Don't blame me, the corporation made the decision!" "It's not my fault; Washington gave the go-ahead!" "The structure of this bureaucracy is such that it precludes me or anyone from making a real decision. I put in my two cents' worth and so does everyone else. Somewhere along the line, all these strands of responsibility get woven together and a decision emerges for which no identifiable person is responsible." According to Thompson, the main defect of this interpretation of collective responsibility, better described as collective nonresponsibility, is that it overlooks what is obvious; namely, that people act in the context of ongoing institutions, and that they "may be culpable for creating the structural faults of the institution, or for making inadequate efforts to correct them."[15]

What Thompson is arguing is similar to what B. F. Skinner points out in *Beyond Freedom and Dignity*. No sooner does Skinner insist that the environment controls us, that he reminds us that the environment is largely of our "own making."[16] Thus bureaucrats need not be passive victims of their bureaucratic environment. They can, if they so choose, respin the bureaucratic web within which they are entangled. For example, if William G. Ouchi is correct, Americans can adapt organizational designs that reflect those used in Japan. Whereas "Type J" structures represent an adaptation to the conditions of homogeneity, stability, and collectivism prevalent in Japanese society, "Type A" structures represent a "natural adaptation" to conditions characteristic of American society: heterogeneity, mobility, and individualism.[17] Nevertheless, an American corporation may, if it so chooses, pattern itself on the "Type J" model. Should it do so, it will create an organizational structure (termed "Type Z" by Ouchi) that will foster conditions of homogeneity, stability, and collectivism—if not in America at large, then at least among the organization's workers. Once such conditions have been established, the notion of collective responsibility—interpreted by Ouchi to mean that state of affairs in which each individual is accountable for every decision and action of the collectivity—is likely to take root and flourish.

Although the notion of collective responsibility seems to broaden and deepen the individual's sense of personal responsibility in ways that the hierarchical notion of responsibility either cannot or does not, this may be a somewhat misleading first impression. With some amazement on his part, Ouchi points out that "Type J" employees are comfortable "in not knowing who is responsible for what" since "they know quite clearly that each of them is completely responsible for all tasks, and they share that responsibility jointly."[18] In theory, this sounds ideal. In practice, it falls somewhat outside the boundaries of the Garden of Eden. Not only does this approach sometimes leave things undone because everyone thinks that "George is doing it," it frequently leads people to adopt the psychology of the contented committee member who is able to solve any pricks of conscience with the balm of "It must be okay because the group says it is okay." "We're in this together" is a consoling motto, but it can cause individuals to forget just how much or how little they contributed to a collective decision.

The Personal Model of Responsibility. If the above line of reasoning is correct, then neither the hierarchical nor the collective model of responsibility is without flaw, especially insofar as those who are located in the bowels of the bureaucracy are concerned. For the most part, the typical policy expert is not a high-level government official, but a struggling economist, biochemist, mathematician, psychologist, or sociologist who makes his or her living gathering and processing the information top-ranking policymakers need in order to make informed decisions. Because there is a natural tendency for lower-level policy experts to downplay their role in the policy process (e.g., "We're technicians, not politicians" or "We're teamplayers, not bosses"), both the hierarchical and the collective models of responsibility seriously undermine the typical policy expert's sense of personal responsibility. For this reason, what Dennis F. Thompson terms a "personal" model of responsibility may be the most appropriate paradigm for policy experts, be they analysts, advisers, or subject-area specialists.

According to Thompson's personal model of responsibility, a policy analyst, for example, is morally responsible for an outcome to the degree that (1) the analyst's actions or omissions cause the outcome; and (2) these actions or omissions are done neither "in ignorance" nor "under compulsion."[19] A person is causally responsible for X to the degree that had he not done Y (where Y is either an action or omission), X would not have occurred. A person is volitionally responsible for X both to the degree that he knew what he was doing in doing X and to the degree that he was physically and psychologically able either to do X or not to do X. Thus, a policy analyst is causally responsible for her report either in the sense that because she wrote and submitted it to the relevant policymakers, it could and probably did contribute to their policy decision; or in the sense that because she did not write and submit it to the relevant policymakers, it could not play a role in their deliberations. Likewise, a policy analyst is volitionally responsible for her report both to the degree that she knew what she was writing when she wrote it and to the degree that it was within her physical and psychological capacity either to write or not to write it.

Causal Excuses for Personal Responsibility. No matter how strongly they are asserted, however, ascriptions of causal and volitional responsibility can be defeated, or at least deflated, provided that the person held responsible for an outcome has a compelling causal or volitional excuse for having caused it.[20] Chief among the causal excuses, according to Thompson, are the excuse from alternative cause and the excuse from null cause. The excuse from alternative cause runs as follows: "If I hadn't done it, someone else would have" or "If I don't do it, someone else will."[21] In its strong form, the excuse has little force, since I can never be certain that my hypothetical replacement would in fact choose to act in situation X as I chose to act in situation X. However, in a weaker form, this excuse may have some validity. Here the policy analyst claims not that someone else would have written just as mediocre a report as he, or succumbed to political pressure as quickly as he; but that someone else would have written an even worse report than he, or succumbed to political pressure even more rapidly than he.

Bernard Williams describes a case involving an appeal to the weakened version of the excuse from alternative cause in *Utilitarianism: For and Against.* A biochemist with heavy family responsibilities finds that the job market in his field is very limited. Finally he is offered a job in a company that does research in chemical and biological warfare. Somewhat of a humanitarian, George objects to that kind of research, but his wife begs him to take the job for her sake and that of the children. It's either this job, the welfare line, or marginal employment as a dishwasher. In the course of mulling over his options, George discovers that if he fails to take the research job, the company is likely to hire another candidate, a brilliant young chemist who may make a major contribution to germ warfare, the kind of contribution George knows that he, George, a run-of-the-mill biochemist, is highly unlikely to make.[22] According to the excuse from alternative cause, George should take the job on the grounds that his rival is likely to commit worse wrongs than George. Humanity is better off if plebeian rather than brilliant biochemists work for warmongering companies. George does us all a service by taking the job. We are spared the evil genius of his rival. Although this excuse may be acceptable to many, it is not acceptable to Williams, who insists that George should refuse the job. If he fails to do so, he will erode his personal integrity. Gradually he will destroy his image of himself as a humanitarian. Once this happens, George will pose a threat to us all, for he will pursue his research not caring which of us or which of our children is struck down with a cruel virus. Despite the force of Williams's objection to the excuse from alternative cause, integrity may not be too high a price to pay at all times and in all places. Ideological purity can degenerate into smug self-righteousness. There are circumstances under which the lesser of two evils may indeed be morally excusable. "Better a *compassionate* slave foreman than a *cruel* one" is very likely the motto not only of the fundamentally decent man who accepts such a job, but of the slaves who must work under him.

The second causal excuse Thompson identifies, the excuse from null cause, is probably more problematic than the first. Here the policy expert exlaims: "Don't blame me. I'm a mere cog in the wheel. The consequential decisions are all made by the big shots." In an analysis of B. F. Goodrich's falsification of test data for the brakes of the Air Force A-7D airplane, Robert Jackall voices an objection to this excuse. About to manufacture test data *ex nihilo* to support a structurally flawed brake system, one engineering supervisor stated: "After all, we're just drawing some curves, and what happens to them after they leave here, well, we're not responsible for that."[23] According to Jackall, this excuse is unacceptable because, like it or not, the supervisor cannot remove himself from the causal chain. If he knows that his falsified data will be used to convince the Air Force that the A-7D airplane is safe, then he is partially responsible for whatever accidents occur. The supervisor cannot extract himself from the causal chain of responsibility simply because he doesn't have final say in a project, or because those who have more say than he does are free either to accept or to reject his data.

Volitional Excuses for Personal Responsibility. When a causal excuse is inappropriate, an agent may appeal to what Thompson terms a volitional excuse, an excuse based on one or both of two factors: absence of intention and/or presence of compulsion.

Absence of Intention. An act is intentional if it meets at least one of the following two conditions: (1) A person *consciously desires* the outcome of his/her act, whatever the likelihood of that outcome may be; or (2) a person knows (subjectively) that the outcome of his/her act is practically certain to follow from his/her conduct, whatever his/her conscious desire may be as to that outcome. Thus, if Defense Department analyst #1 consciously desires President Reagan to act upon her recommendations for adding weapons to our nuclear stockpile, then she acts intentionally whatever the likelihood of Reagan's acting upon her recommendation may be. Or if Defense Department analyst #2 knows that President Reagan is practically certain to use her statistics to justify an increase in our nuclear stockpile, she acts intentionally in handing over her statistics to the President even if she has no conscious desire that her statistics be used in this way. Because both analysts #1 and #2 have acted intentionally, we will hold them at least partially responsible for the direct or indirect harmful outcomes of their actions. In contrast, we are not prone to hold a policy analyst responsible for the harmful outcomes of his or her nonintentional actions. So, for example, if an HEW analyst has neither a conscious desire to submit a recommendation that aid to dependent children be terminated nor practically certain knowledge that his work will be used to justify such a termination, then we will not automatically blame him should HEW decide to discontinue its support of needy children. However, we may come to blame him at least partially for the cut if we discover that there were steps he both could and should have taken to figure out for what ends his work would be used. Willful blindness is no excuse for lack of foresight. When policy experts, or policymakers for that matter, make themselves the "instruments of their own ignorance"[24] by blithely adopting the motto, "See no evil, hear no evil, speak no evil," we excuse their lack of foresight at the risk of encouraging an atmosphere of deliberate moral benightedness.

Presence of Compulsion. In addition to the volitional excuse based on lack of ignorance is the one based on presence of coercion. Here the policy expert pleads that an individual—or more abstractedly, an institution—made him or her "feel compelled to do something he or she would not normally do."[25] The paradigm case of coercion is, of course, the use of physical force or psychological constraint. In addition, not only threats of physical force or psychological constraint, but even some offers of physical or psychological rewards are coercive, albeit to a lesser degree. So, for example, if the Secretary of Defense threatens to fire an analyst unless he comes up with a quantitative justification for building bigger and "better" bombs, then that analyst may feel compelled to fudge data—something he normally would not do. We should note, however, that if the Secretary of Defense adopts another strategy and promises to reward the analyst with a promotion for fudging the requisite data, that analyst will not necessarily feel any less compelled to do that which he normally would not do. Bribes are not necessarily less coercive than threats; kind offers that meet resistance easily mutate into cruel threats.

Institutional Coercion
Versus Individual Responsibility

For reasons that will become apparent shortly, excuses based on "individual coercion" are far less threatening to our convictions about personal responsibility than excuses based on "institutional coercion." Although the concept of institutional coercion is a recent and somewhat jarring addition to the pantheon of volitional excuses, it has been welcomed as a needed moral innovation by many. Radical feminists, for example, have made good use of this concept in the course of arguing that, in our culture, women are made to feel compelled to have sexual intercourse with men—something they would not automatically do in another, less male-dominated, culture. Coercion, these feminists claim, is not confined to instances of *individual coercion* ranging from a particular man's deliberate threatening of a woman ("Pull up your dress and don't scream, or I'll kill you") to his plying her with drugs or alcohol ("Soon she won't have the will to resist). Rather, coercion also embraces cases of *institutional coercion* that proceed from the general structure of heterosexual relations in this culture—a culture that discourages women from asserting themselves both in the private and public spheres, and that encourages women to submit to all of men's demands, but especially to their sexual demands:

> Women, constantly propositioned by men and even manhandled (the phrase is no accident), are trained to feel that they must be gentle and inoffensive in their rejections. This conditioning, which makes many women afraid or incapable of opposing men (the woman's marriage vow runs, significantly, "love, honor, and obey"), also reduces the verbal and physical forcefulness of their resistance, and it is thus easy for men to ignore or mistake their meaning, with disastrous consequences to the woman.[26]

That many men think women are saying "yes," when in fact they are saying "no" to rape is apparent. Nevertheless, to deny that the forces of institutional coercion make it impossible for men ever to get women's signals straight may be to overstate the case. Patriarchal institutions may narrow, limit, impede, constrain, and constrict women's choices as sexual beings without determining women's choices as sexual beings.[27] There is, after all, a significant difference between claiming that women's sexual wants and needs are shaped by their culture, and insisting that no individual woman can ever break the mold culture initially imposes upon their sexual wants and needs.

In this connection Judith Butler comments:

> If our desires and fantasies are informed by surrounding culture, does this mean that we are thoroughly subject to the political realities responsible for this "construction"? What sense can we make of sexual choice if our sexuality is itself a product of external forces? It feels to me that if we are all determined by the existing social and political order, then we are all in a sense the dominant culture's masochists. And I'm not sure I want to play that role.[28]

In other words, if the notion of institutional coercion is overemphasized, all real choice is impossible—including the choice of women to change the structures of society in ways that discourage women from being perennial victims, men from being continual predators, and sexual relations from being fundamentally coercive. Therefore, if women wish to think of themselves as agents who can make a difference, it may be in their best interests to regard the forces of institutional coercion as surmountable in ways that the forces of individual coercion are not. No matter how overwhelming the power of city hall may seem, it can be fought in ways that a nasty blackmailer cannot.[29]

The point of this digression is first to agree with those who have argued that the ethos of the institution shapes in its employees·"a strong orientation to their bureaucracy's goals, habits of careful calculation, and a distrust of intangible issues of value which threaten to disrupt the calculated achievement of goals,"[30] and second to disagree with those who have insisted that there is nothing that we, or anybody else, can do to alter this state of affairs. Unless we let the institutions with which we are associated mold us, we cannot hope to survive in them—let alone thrive in them.

That institutions—or bureaucracies, as they are sometimes called—are able to shape their employees' attitudes, beliefs, and actions is a point we need not belabor. It is not, however, as if policy experts, for example, are asked to sign a pledge to do everything in their power to make the institution bloom and grow. On the contrary! The process whereby their consciences are taken over by the institution's ethos is far more insidious than this for at least three reasons.

First, policy experts can do only so many cost-effectiveness, cost-benefit, and risk-benefit analyses before they start to see the world in terms of dollar signs, or in terms of hedons (units of pleasure) and dolors (units of pain). Second, policy experts can speak the neutral language of the bureaucrat only so long before a moral numbness occurs. The operations researcher, who is initially distressed by his role in the destruction of human life, gains peace of mind by calling bombs "ordnance," bombing "interdiction," the cultural extirpation of thousands of people "pacification," and defoliation "a resources control program."[31] Third, policy experts can stay buried in the bureaucracy only so long before they begin to separate themselves from the consequences of their actions.

That all of the above forces are indeed working on the policy expert's psyche became clear to me during a meeting I had with several Washington, D.C., policy analysts. One analyst told me that what I needed to understand was the fact that he dealt with millions of people and billions of dollars. He argued that because he never came into direct contact with the people who had been negatively affected by his policy recommendations, he was somehow not responsible for the harm that had befallen them either as the result of his negligent, reckless, or intentional miscalculations or as the consequence of his decision to maximize aggregate utility at the expense of individual rights.

At first I was appalled by the analyst's reasoning: "You're not responsible for what you don't see." I wondered how an intelligent person could make such a foolish statement. Then I recalled that the two bases of any bureaucracy's efficiency, segmentation and specialization, separate people from their work. Segmentation, the breaking of tasks into small parts to obtain speed, separates experts from the final product of their effort; and specialization, the demand for exhaustive but narrow expertise on some aspect of a problem, separates experts from the use to which their knowledge is put. One analyst may be responsible for one input (the effect of an oil embargo on the automobile industry), another for another type of input (the effect on steel industry investment), another for another type of input (the effect on consumer purchase of automobile gasoline and home heating oil). Until the team leader puts the inputs together, the parts of the analysis will certainly not equal the whole. And even when the whole report is put together and sent to the relevant policymaker, chances are that neither the team leader nor the team members will have any clear sense about the fate of their report.

This structural compartmentalization, where means and ends, actions and consequences are divorced, often leads to a parallel psychic compartmentalization where personal responsibility for action is lost somewhere in the bureaucratic maze. Arnold Meltsner suggests that at least three things can be done to break down psychic compartmentalization and to increase personal responsibility: (1) Analysts should be encouraged to consider implementation concerns when defining the problem and presenting their recommendations; (2) clients should hold their analysts responsible for what happens in the field or at least judge them by results in practice and not merely by what they produce on paper; and (3) where possible, the analysts should obtain feedback, negative and positive, from those whose lives have been affected by their estimates, projections, and so on.[32]

Of these three suggestions, the third gets to the heart of the matter. Writing on the teaching of ethics in a pluralistic society, Peter Caws reiterates Meltsner's point poignantly:

> I remember, during the Vietnam War, being in a plane somewhere between Los Angeles and New York, and noticing what must have been a fire in a house or barn some 30,000 feet below. I had a sudden sense of what it might have been like for a flyer to have started that fire by a well-placed bomb—the pride he might have taken in the accuracy of the ballistics involved, as a remote puff of smoke testified to an impersonal target successfully annihilated. The unreality of pain and death at such a distance made me reflect on how easy it is to neutralize the moral sentiments . . . . But I believe that along with rational convictions about moral behavior there must always go, in some form or other, an identification with the particular persons who are affected by this behavior, if the situation is to be morally alive, as it were. . . . I also believe that this identification is naturally produced by close acquaintance, along with information about the state of the affected persons, and that this leads to morally reflective responses except in cases where for professional or pathological reasons the sympathetic reaction is suppressed.[33]

That Caws is not alone in his reflections is clear. Robert Jackall reports that when thalidomide had wreaked its havoc—hundreds of stillborn infants and thousands of severely defective infants—one of the executives of Giüinenthal, a company that had aggressively marketed thalidomide, saw pictures of some thalidomide children and became nauseated. Jackall goes on to wonder "what would have happened had such a confrontation taken place earlier."[34] Would Giüinenthal have taken thalidomide off the market voluntarily? Would the inventors, manufacturers, and marketers of thalidomide have understood the awful consequences of their product? If so, then Caws is on the right track when he urges us to build into the teaching of professional ethics, as far as this is possible, a firsthand and personal acquaintance with the classes of persons likely to be affected by one's professional decisions.[35]

PRACTICES VERSUS INSTITUTION

Prevailing institutional (bureaucratic) structures do indeed militate against some of our most treasured notions of personal responsibility. But the solution is not to destroy our institutions, which, after all, make possible a quality of life most of us

. F. Skinner, *Beyond Freedom and Dignity* (New York: Bantam/Vintage Books, 1972),

illiam G. Ouchi, *Theory Z* (New York: Avon Books, 1981), 56.

id.

hompson, "Moral Responsibility of Public Officials," 908.

id., 909-914.

id., 909.

J. C. Smart and Bernard Williams, *Utilitiarianism: For and Against* (New York: Cam-
iversity Press, 1973), 97-99.

obert Jackall, "Structural Invitations to Deceit: Some Reflections on Bureaucracy and
" in *Berkshire Review*, special issue on *Lying and Deception* 15 (1980), 55.

hompson, "Moral Responsibility of Public Officials," 912.

hn C. Hughes and Larry May, "Sexual Harassment," *Social Theory and Practice* 6
)), 251.

lia Melani and Linda Fodaski, "The Psychology of the Rapist and His Victim," in
e First Sourcebook eds. Noreen Cornell and Cassandra Wilson (New York: New Amer-
ry, Plenum Press, 1974), 89.

id., 49.

dith Butler, review of *Diary of a Conference on Sexuality, Gay Community News* 9
r 1981), 6.

r further analysis of this point see Rosemarie Tong, *Women, Sex and the Law*
N.J.: Rowman and Allenheld, 1984), 109-11.

ckall, "Structural Invitations to Deceit," 52.

id., 53.

rnold J. Meltsner, *Policy Analysts in the Bureaucracy* (Berkeley: University of Califor-
1976), 151.

ter Caws, "On the Teaching of Ethics in a Pluralistic Society," *The Hastings Center*
no. 5 (October 1978), 39.

ckall, "Structural Invitations to Deceit," 56.

ws, "On the Teaching of Ethics in a Pluralistic Society," 39.

asdair MacIntyre, *After Virtue* (Notre Dame, Ind.: University of Notre Dame Press,
.

d., 178.

d., 181.

d.

nold J. Meltsner, "Creating a Policy Analysis Profession," *Society* 16, no. 6 (Septem-
er 1979), 51.

are not prepared to forsake. Rather, it is to shape our institutions so that their structures can support us in our efforts to achieve the good life. In this connection, Alasdair MacIntyre makes an excellent distinction between what he terms a "practice" and what he terms an "institution."

A practice is, according to MacIntyre, a cooperative human activity that has its own standards of excellence. These practices include everything from game playing (chess, football, tennis) to professional activities like medicine, law, and teaching to personal activities like parenting. If any of these practices are to flourish, then their practitioners must appreciate those satisfactions or goods internal to them. For example, consider the practice of teaching. What makes teaching worthwhile for me are the intellectual challenges it provides and the human relationships it fosters. I became a teacher because I was attracted to a life devoted to the accumulation and sharing of knowledge, one of those rare human goods of which there is—at least in principle—enough to go around. The fact that I own a particular house means that you cannot also own it; but the fact that I know Plato's *Dialogues* in no way prevents you and millions of others from also knowing them.

There is, however, more to teaching than the *possession* of the goods internal to it. There is the *achievement* of those goods, a process that involves standards of excellence and obedience to rules. Comments MacIntyre:

> To enter into a practice is to accept the authority of those standards and the inadequacy of my own performance as judged by them. It is to subject my own attitudes, choices, preferences and tastes to the standards which currently and partially define the practice.[36]

Thus, when I decided to become a teacher of philosophy, I knew that I would be judged by a set of performance criteria established by reigning luminaries in the field, and that I would have to give up certain idiosyncratic notions both of philosophy and of teaching in order to become a recognizable member of the community of philosophy teachers.

To enter into the transforming process of becoming an excellent philosophy teacher, however, is one thing; to persevere in the process is quite another. According to MacIntyre, none of us can persevere in a practice long enough to achieve its internal goods without the requisite virtues or acquired human qualities that enable us to keep striving on those days when it does not seem worth it. Anyone engaged in a human practice—be it tennis playing, doctoring, lawyering, analyzing, advising, or, as in my case, teaching—knows how hard it is to become excellent at that which one has chosen to do. Among other things, observes MacIntyre:

> We have to learn to recognize what is due to whom; we have to be prepared to take whatever self-endangering risks are demanded along the way; and we have to listen carefully to what we are told about our own inadequacies and to reply with the same carefulness for the facts. In other words we have to accept as necessary components of any practice with internal goods and standards of excellence the virtues of justice, courage and honesty.[37]

Insofar as teaching goes, for example, justice consists of fulfilling one's obligations to students, to colleagues, and to the profession; courage consists in articulating a new idea or devising a novel teaching method even if such innovations go unrewarded or are penalized; and honesty consists in realizing one's own limits as a teacher as well as the limits of others. As abstract as this may sound, any teacher who has tried to meet *all* of his or her professional obligations without cutting any corners, to mount an experimental course of studies only to fail miserably at it, or to accept a deserved tenure rejection knows of what I speak.

Virtuous practitioners—just, courageous, and honest men and women—are a necessary condition for a practice's survival. But they are not a sufficient condition. "No practices," proclaims MacIntyre, "can survive for any length of time unsustained by institutions."[38] Although some of us may identify practices like teaching, business, medicine, and tennis playing with institutions like colleges, corporations, hospitals, and tennis clubs, such identifications are to be resisted. Practices are characteristically concerned with what we have been terming internal goods—for example, the joy of teaching—and they are held together by the sealing cement of human cooperation. In contrast, institutions are necessarily concerned with so-called external goods like money, power, and status—for example, a salary of $150,000 per annum—and they are energized by the fragmentary fires of human competition. But, continues MacIntyre, this is not only the way it is, but also the way it ought to be, provided that "the ideals and the creativity of the practice" do not succumb to "the acquisitiveness of the institution."[39]

What is refreshing about MacIntyre's analysis of institutions (bureaucracies) is that he finds a worthy place for them in his system despite some of their negative features. Philosophy teachers would still be peripatetic intellectuals were it not for the advent of the academy. Williams College, for example, provides me with the material support I need to teach philosophy. Admittedly, I could teach philosophy without the support of Williams College, or any other educational institution, for that matter, but it would not be easy. Very few of my philosopher friends who lack institutional support have been able to survive, let alone to thrive as teachers. Most of them have given up the struggle; it is simply too difficult to go it alone as a philosophy teacher. Moreover, I very much doubt that the teaching of philosophy could continue in a recognizable form were all philosophers ousted from institutions of higher learning. Nevertheless, despite the fact that practices are symbiotically related to institutions, it is important to remember that all institutions are ruled by the sign of Gemini: to the degree that an institution can support a practice, it can also distort it. For example, to the degree that Williams College provides me with an adequate salary, professional contacts, bright students, engaged colleagues, and sabbatical leaves, it enables me to develop as an excellent teacher. But to the degree that Williams College encourages me to go for the gold or to pursue glory—to be not the best teacher but the most highly paid or the most well-known teacher—it inhibits my growth as an excellent teacher. The best teachers teach not for fame and fortune, but for the intellectual joy of sharing knowledge.

Like teaching, policy analyzing, advising, and consulting are practices embedded in the bureaucratic or institutional structure we sometimes call government. Significantly, the public often fails to realize that policy expertise is a bona fide practice,

tending to identify it either with a set of mere technical [...] tions that support it. That those who work as policy expe[...] pation as a practice, however, is clearly stated by Arnol[...] wishes to see policy analysis and its cognate fields devel[...] this

> . . . means developing common curriculum and sta[...]
> means intellectual exchange and controversy. It me[...]
> ety of ways of openly communicating with each ot[...]
> newsletters—to improve performance and to criti[...]
> and elites.[40]

Without internal standards of excellence (i.e., the abili[...] the state of the art) and without internal goods (i.e., t[...] that, as the result of one's expertise, the policies that gov[...] likely to effect a humane social order), policy analyzir[...] cannot develop into a mature practice. But with these[...] with a conception of themselves as just, courageous, an[...] perts will be able not only to perfect their practice b[...] framework (institution creating and sustaining is, after [...] mit them to make a major contribution to the so-cal[...] makes it all worthwhile for each and every one of us.

NOTES

1. Niccolò Machiavelli, *The Prince*, trans. George Bull (B[...] 96–98.

2. Max Weber, "Politics as a Vocation," in *From Max [...] Hans H. Gerth and C. Wright Mills (New York: Oxford Universi[...]

3. Michael Walzer, "Political Action: The Problem of Dirt[...] *Affairs* 2, no. 2 (Winter 1973), 161.

4. Ibid., 165–67.

5. For a detailed discussion of "dirty hands," see Peter [...] (Englewood Cliffs, N.J.: Prentice-Hall, Inc., 1983), 15–24.

6. Walzer, "Political Action: The Problem of Dirty Hands[...]

7. Ibid., 167.

8. Alan H. Goldman, *The Moral Foundations of Profess[...] man and Littlefield, 1980), 71–72.

9. Ibid., 67.

10. David Luban, "Professional Ethics in a World witho[...] *Report* 11, no. 3 (June 1981), 40.

11. Dennis F. Thompson, "Moral Responsibility of Publi[...] Hands," *The American Political Science Review* 74, no. 4 (De[...]

12. Ibid.

13. Ibid., 907.

14. Ibid.

15. Ibid., 908.

16. [...]
205.

17. [...]

18. I[...]

19. [...]

20. I[...]

21. I[...]

22. J[...]
bridge U[...]

23. R[...]
Morality,[...]

24. T[...]

25. J[...]
(Fall 198[...]

26. L[...]
Rape: Th[...]
ican Libra[...]

27. Ib[...]

28. Ju[...]
(Decembe[...]

29. F[...]
(Totowa,[...]

30. Ja[...]

31. Ib[...]

32. A[...]
nia Press,[...]

33. Pe[...]
Report 8,[...]

34. Ja[...]

35. Ca[...]

36. Al[...]
1981), 17[...]

37. Ib[...]

38. Ib[...]

39. Ib[...]

40. Ar[...]
ber/Octob[...]

Chapter 5

Toward an Ethics for Policy Experts

The preceding chapters have clarified the complex world of policy experts who must accept responsibility for their analyses, advisings, and advocacies. The questions addressed in this and in the next three chapters are more specifically ethical. What I wish to avoid in Chapters 6 through 8 is the smorgasbord effect—a sampling of deontological, utilitarian, libertarian, and contractarian views about policy experts' obligations to clients, third parties, and their profession. Although such an approach is informative, it leaves us with the impression that policy experts are free to pick and choose among ethical theories, discarding those that prove unpalatable. It also leaves us with the impression that morality is about rules, rules, and more rules. For these reasons, without denying the important role that rules play in the moral life, I will argue that unless we understand the role virtues play in the moral life, our ethics will be more cosmetic than efficacious. I will also argue that although all of us must acquire a minimal set of virtues if we are to achieve ethical maturity, professionals must also cultivate those virtues specific to their occupations if they are to execute their tasks in a morally commendable manner. But before I make either of these arguments, I wish both to describe in general what rule-dominated ethical theories are and how they differ from virtue-guided theories, and to explain in detail Aristotle's theory of virtue from which many of my insights are drawn.

RULE-DOMINATED ETHICAL THEORIES VERSUS VIRTUE-GUIDED ETHICAL THEORIES

The Ethics of Rules

Compared with the ethics of virtue which is concerned primarily with an individual's character, the ethics of rules is concerned primarily with an individual's conduct or actions. Throughout the centuries, philosophers have wondered whether there is some one supreme principle of morality from which all our moral rules can be derived. Although various principles have been articulated, none of them have dominated the moral landscape as much as those suggested by utilitarianism and deontology.

Utilitarianism. According to the utilitarian, an act is morally right if and only if it brings about the greatest happiness for the greatest number of people. Thus, in order to decide what he or she ought to do, the utilitarian needs to consider both the happiness-producing (good) and unhappiness-producing (bad) consequences of alternative actions A_1, A_2, A_3, A_n. Whatever alternative is likely to produce the most overall *net* happiness (good minus bad; benefit minus cost) is the action he or she ought to do.

Utilitarianism seems both intuitively appealing and refreshingly straightforward until we start asking questions about it. What is happiness? Why ought we pursue it? And even if we ought to pursue our own separate happinesses, why ought we pursue the happiness of the "greatest number of people"? Stated abstractly, happiness is the *intrinsic* good, desired for itself, whereas all other goods are merely *instrumental* goods, desired only insofar as they contribute to happiness. Depending on whether one is a hedonistic utilitarian, a pluralistic utilitarian, or a preference utilitarian, however, this intrinsic good will assume a variety of meanings. For the hedonistic utilitarian, happiness is synonymous with pleasure, be that pleasure mental or physical; for the pluralistic utilitarian, happiness is to be identified not with one end good but with a multiplicity of end goods like knowledge, love, and beauty; and for the preference utilitarian, happiness is whatever each individual prefers to obtain.

Of these three versions of utilitarianism, preference utilitarianism is best able to handle so-called interpersonal comparisons of utility. Whereas it is extremely difficult first to measure how much happiness (pleasure) Joe is getting from wine, women, and song and how much happiness (pleasure) Sam is getting from *no* wine, women, or song, and then to compare Joe's and Sam's respective levels of happiness (pleasure) in order to decide which is quantitatively greater, it is relatively easy to measure Joe's preference for indulgence over abstinence and Sam's preference for abstinence over indulgence. All we need do is ask Joe and Sam about their preferences. Nevertheless, preference utilitarianism is flawed to the degree that it is unable to handle so-called "unacceptable desires." Since preference utilitarians do not want to defend a policy of genocide on the grounds that Nazis prefer a world without Jews to a world with Jews, they will have to provide criteria for distinguishing between acceptable and unacceptable preferences. If preference utilitarians tell us that an acceptable preference is a rational preference, then we stubborn questioners will probably ask them to distinguish between rational and irrational preferences. Despite the fact that hundreds of philosophers are working on this problem, however, their efforts have yet to yield a set of necessary and sufficient conditions for rationality. Therefore, any attempt to define an acceptable preference as a rational preference is not particularly illuminating.

Even if philosophers were able to distinguish between rational and irrational preferences, however, the preference utilitarian—like the hedonistic and pluralistic utilitarian—would have to convince us that we have an obligation to maximize the corporate happiness even at the expense of our own individual happinesses. In the nineteenth century, Bentham appealed to our *egoistic* tendencies, claiming that it is in our own self-interest to promote everyone's interest, whereas Mill, his disciple, appealed to our *altruistic* tendencies or social feelings. We have, said Mill, what amounts to a natural but very limited animal sympathy for members of our species (we grimace, for example, when we see one of our own tortured), and it is the purpose of morality to promote these natural sympathies and to fight their limitations. As persuasive as these two lines of reasoning seem, neither of them is effective in meeting the objections of a self-sufficient, smug, and unsympathetic egoist who always attains all that he needs and wants without ever taking into account anyone's happiness but his own. In all fairness to Bentham and Mill, however, if the egoist is not convinced by their rationale for being moral, he or she is not likely to be convinced by anyone else's either.

Assuming for the sake of argument that most of us are not hardhearted egoists but warm-blooded utilitarians, eager to follow those rules which, if followed by everyone, would in general maximize happiness, all of us may agree, for example, to tell the truth. A society in which people routinely lied to one another would be unlivable. Nevertheless, despite our basic agreement, the so-called act utilitarians among us would regard the rule "Tell the truth" as a mere thumb rule that circumstances could easily defeat. "Always tell the truth unless, in the circumstances, you can better maximize aggregate utility by lying," proclaims the act utilitarian. In contrast, the so-called rule utilitarians among us will insist that the rule "Tell the truth" is not easily—if ever—defeated. "Always tell the truth even if, in the short run, it appears that lying would better maximize aggregate utility," proclaims the rule utilitarian. But, we may wonder, is the rule utilitarian appealing to the "long run" because he or she believes that as a matter of empirical fact, lying won't ultimately maximize aggregate utility? Or because he or she is a closet deontologist (see following section on deontology) according to whom lying is always wrong, even on those occasions when lying does, as a matter of empirical fact, maximize aggregate utility? In either event, the rule utilitarian has to cope with our suspicion that no one knows enough about the long run to base any moral claims upon it whatsoever.

Our discussion of act and rule utilitarianism brings into focus the problem that most jeopardizes the utilitarian project; namely, its apparent willingness to sacrifice the rights of a few to achieve the happiness of the many. Suppose, for example, that we could increase the GNP tenfold by enslaving a small group of people—the technologically skilled, for example. Even if the enslaved people were treated decently, some of us would protest that it is wrong to deprive a select few of their liberty in order to maximize the majority's standard of living. Although the act utilitarian has no real way of meeting this objection short of proclaiming that the liberty of the few has greater utility-value than the combined material comforts of the many (a proclamation difficult to prove), the rule utilitarian can, as just noted, argue that in the long run a policy of enslavement will not maximize utility. The slaves will eventually revolt and cause social chaos; as a result, the GNP will plummet as never before. But, we may wonder, what if the slaves were "programmed" never to revolt? Would that make their captivity any less wrong or more right? Is there not something intrinsically wrong about enslaving a person no matter what his or her enslavement nets in terms of aggregate utility?

Deontology. It is this question and the answer to it that serves as a transition to our discussion of deontology (from the Greek work for duty), especially Kant's version of it. As mentioned above, according to utilitarian theory we might be justified in enslaving a few people (thus harming them) if by doing this we could bring about enough overall happiness to outweigh the unhappiness of the persons harmed. The end, it seems, would justify the means. In contrast, respect for individual human persons is key in Kantian theory. One must never treat another person merely as a means.

A second contrast between utilitarianism and Kant's deontology is that the former is a consequentialist ethical theory, whereas the latter is a nonconsequentialist ethical theory. Unlike the utilitarians who insist that what makes an action right or wrong is its felicific consequences, Kant maintains that an action is morally worthy or morally unworthy depending on one's reasons for doing it. What makes an action morally worthy is that I perform it from duty rather than merely in accord with duty. If I jump into a swimming pool and save a drowning child simply because my heart goes out to the tot or simply in order to collect a reward, then I am merely in accord with duty. In contrast, if I plunge into the chilly waters from a sense of duty—because I adhere to the valid moral rule "Save a human life whenever you are able to do so"—then my action is morally worthy. As Kant sees it, human inclinations as different as warmheartedness and greed are not a firm foundation for moral action. Today the sun is shining and everything is going great for me. Because my heart is full of love for one and all, I probably won't hesitate to put myself out for you. But catch me on a rainy day after my boss has just fired me, and you'll find my heart as cold as a lump of wet coal. Chances are that I'll ignore your pleas for help. Precisely because inclinations are so changeable, Kant insists that rationality is the ground of morality. Reason, and reason alone, transcends the contingencies of space and time. Whether the day brings sunshine or rain, reason will instruct me to save any drowning child that I can. Would it be wrong for me to save a drowning child simply because I have a real soft spot for kids? Here Kant would say that although the consequences of my inclination-based actions are good (beneficial), the action itself is wrong in the sense of being morally unworthy of a rational person. Apparently, the disciple of Kant and the typical utilitarian mean something quite different by the terms "right" and "wrong."

These two points of contrast bring Kant's deontology into focus. According to Kant, an action is right when it is done from duty. And an action is wrong either when it flaunts duty or when it is done merely in accord with duty, as when a shopkeeper gives the correct change not because he is motivated to obey the valid moral rule "Be honest," but merely because he wants a good reputation in the community.

All this talk of obeying the law makes Kant sound like a rule utilitarian except that for Kant a valid moral rule is not a rule that necessarily has good consequences, but rather is one that meets the test of the so-called categorical imperative. The categorical imperative has three formulations:

1. Act only on that maxim through which you can at the same time will that it should become a universal law;
2. Act in such a way that you always treat humanity, whether in your own person or in the person of another, never simply as a means but always at the same time as an end; and
3. Never . . . perform an action except on a maxim such as can also be a universal law, and consequently such that the will can regard itself as at the same time making universal law by its maxim.[1]

If an action is not consistently universalizable in the sense that a rational human being could will that anyone use the principle to determine his or her actions, an instance of treating all involved persons as ends in themselves or intrinsically valuable beings, and self-imposed by one's own rational will, then it is morally wrong irrespective of its beneficial consequences.

The categorical imperative summarizes, however abstractly, the substance of Kant's theory. It tells us what general rules to use in deciding what to do. But it does not tell us why we should follow it. Kant argues that we all do use this threefold test or the like in estimating the morality of acts. If happiness were the highest good for human persons, as the utilitarians suggest, then, says Kant, we would have been better designed without minds. Blind instinct, programmed to achieve its felicific goal no matter what, would have suited us better. Reason is a spoilsport that routinely deflects our appetites from going where they would go were they left to their own devices. Now, Kant is not upset by the way we have in fact been structured. He counts it as a plus rather than a minus that we differ from all other terrestrial beings insofar as we have a capacity for rationality. The behavior of all other beings—animate as well as inanimate—is determined simply by laws of nature. Rocks do not decice to fall; they fall by virtue of the law of gravity. Lions do not decide to mate; they mate by virtue of certain sexual drives over which they have no control. In contrast, we are not entirely determined by externally imposed laws. We have the capacity to make laws for ourselves—to decide how we will act. Thus, insists Kant, our fundamental goal is not to be happy—any sentient creature has this aim—but rather to act autonomously, to free ourselves from the blandishments of our inclinations.

To understand in greater detail not only the differences between Kantianism and utilitarianism, but also the limits of both consequentialist and nonconsequentialist theories of ethics, let us consider a specific case. Suppose a teacher asks her students whether it is right or wrong to discriminate against female professors on account of their sex, to deny them tenure simply because they are women. Because the students are not forthcoming with a quick response, the teacher instructs them to apply both consequentialist and nonconsequentialist ethical theories to the situation. The application yields the following results. First, the students realize that the *act utilitarian* is unable to take an unqualified stand on this or any type of discrimination. If denying a woman professor tenure is calculated to produce more net good for the college than granting her tenure, it is the right action. If not, it is the wrong action. Next, the somewhat disconcerted student discovers that *rule utilitarianism* is also unable to take an unqualified stand on sex discrimination. If following a certain sexist rule like "Do not tenure women even if they are deserving" is calculated to produce more net good than a competing nonsexist rule like "Tenure women if they are deserving," then it is the right rule to follow. If not, it is the wrong rule to follow. Like the calculus of act utilitarianism, the calculus of rule utilitarianism is based not on a rule's intrinsic features but on its instrumental efficacy—its ability to maximize social good. Thus when individual rights and appeals to justice enter into a utilitarian calculation, they do so only on the basis of the consequences that follow upon espousing them as opposed to flaunting them.

Disappointed that utilitarianism is unable to provide unambiguous yes or no answers, the students turn to a purely nonconsequentialist position like Kant's deontology, hoping to find out once and for all whether sex discrimination is right or wrong. Unlike the utilitarian, the Kantian will not justify denying people their due on the basis of the total good netted by an action. A Kantian will look at a practice of sex discrimination to see whether the rule that governs it—"Don't reward deserving people if it proves disutilitarian to do so"—is compatible with all three versions of the categorical imperative. Any such rule is likely to be invalid (irrational, immoral) because, for example, it is an instance of treating one person as a mere means to the happiness of some other persons. A woman who has earned tenure by dint of her hard work is denied tenure simply because it serves the pleasure of the "old boys" who do not like women (very few of whom smoke cigars, drink whiskey, follow the races, or swear like troopers) "moralizing" on the faculty floor.

Relieved that Kantianism is able to enunciate moral rules that are binding under any circumstances—for example, "Reward deserving persons"—the students heave a sigh of relief. "At last we have found an ethical theory with teeth!" The students' moment of elation is short-lived, however. The instructor reminds them that the principle of humanity or even the principle of self-respect, at least as applied by Kant himself, forbids premarital sex, masturbation, and several other actions the contemporary conscience has little trouble justifying. Visibly shaken, the students conclude that ethics is subjective—that there are no objective principles that govern all persons, at all times, and in all places.

The Ethics of Virtue: Focus on Aristotle

There are two basic ways to respond to the charge that ethics is subjective. We can go the way of Nietzsche and insist that ethics is nothing more than the spoutings and spewings of an irrational will that generates its own values. Or we can go the way of Aristotle and accept the fact that ethics is not so much the search for transcendent objective principles that must be obeyed come hell or high water as the exercise of a set of spatially and temporally bound virtues that we may regard as our primary defense system against the destruction or erosion of that human community without which our lives would be aimless.[2]

An ethics that follows Nietzsche's lead would be disastrous in the public policy arena. If the ideas of community, of the common good, and of the public interest are lurking anywhere, then they are lurking in the public policy arena; and if any philosophy is fundamentally noncommunitarian, if not downright anticommunitarian, it is that of Nietzsche. For Nietzsche, there are two moralities: the slave morality, the morality of the common herd, of the "Thou shalts" and the "Thou shalt nots"; and the master morality, the morality of the exceptional individual, of the "*I* shall" and the "*I* shall not."[3] If Nietzsche has any bones to pick with Kant—and he has several—it is Kant's insistence on the *universal* applicability of valid moral rules. Nietzsche refuses to be bound by the legislations of a transcendent, rational will that binds all human persons no matter what their distinguishing features. Rather, Nietzsche abides by the rulings of his empirical ego, in all its uniqueness.

Although many of us might like to proclaim ourselves *übermenschen* (overmen) along with Nietzsche, in order to do so we have to forgo the warmth of human companionship. If we are not prepared to stand literally alone, then we have to submit ourselves to the discipline of life together. Public policymaking may be a leveling process, but the sharp edges of individuality it blunts are the very same edges that would prevent us from creating and maintaining community, a task that is just as risk-taking, challenging, and exhilarating as the *cult*ivation of one's lonely uniqueness.

In contrast to Nietzsche's anticommunitarian ethics, Aristotle's ethics is well suited to the policy arena because, for Aristotle, morality is essentially bound up with bringing about an ultimate human good. Aristotle reasons that all human objectives lead to further objectives until some supreme objective is attained, an ultimate good for the sake of which all other goods are pursued. Aristotle conceives this good as *eudaimonia* (well-being, flourishing, or happiness), "an active life in accord with excellence, or if there are more forms of excellence than one, in accord with the best and completest of them."[4] This supreme excellence is reasoning or intelligence, understood largely as the capacity for rational discourse. We continually talk to ourselves and to others about what we are going to do, when, and why.

Once we focus on *eudaimonia*, then it makes sense to talk about practices, those coherent and complex forms of socially established cooperative human activity we discussed in Chapter 4. If the happy life is the active life, the life in which we exercise our capacities, tendencies, and functions in an unimpeded way, then it is the life of practitioners—persons engaged in as many human practices as they can do well. But it is difficult to learn how to order our separate practical lives and how to cooperate with each other in the living of them. A person may enjoy practices like parenting, golfing, teaching, and filmmaking. How should he or she order these pursuits and relate them to those of others? According to Aristotle, these questions cannot be answered by appeals to the principle of utility or to the categorical imperative. Not even the most sophisticated weighing of hedons (units of pleasure) and dolors (units of pain) can tell a man whether it is good for him to be getting so much pleasure from golfing and so little pleasure from parenting his daughter. Similarly, not even the most scrupulous application of the categorical imperative can tell a woman whether her duties as a wife and mother take precedence over her duties as a scholar and teacher. What will mediate such situations, however, is practical wisdom, intelligence in directing human activities to the end of human well-being.

Practical wisdom has two indispensable functions. First, practical wisdom is the ability not only to know the means to certain desired ends, but also to know what ends are desirable (worthy of desire). The person who is merely clever is able to find the means appropriate to the attainment of many ends, be those ends good or bad. Although the person of practical wisdom is also gifted with this technical skill, he or she exercises it only on behalf of good ends—that is, those ends which, when taken together, properly ranked, and gradually achieved, constitute "what is best" or "the human good." Second, practical wisdom is the *sine qua non* for the proper exercise of all other virtues, and unless we are able to exercise certain requisite virtues, we cannot hope to attain the specific goods internal to any practice or the general good toward which all worthy practices tend—namely, the good of flourishing as an individual in a community. Unless a person is practically wise, he or she will exhibit not virtue X, but either its excess or defect. So, for example, a woman who lacks practical wisdom will not act courageously but either rashly or cowardly. Likewise, the man who lacks practical wisdom will not act in a generous manner but either in a niggardly manner or an ostentatious manner. And so on, for each and every virtue.

The moral genius of the person of practical wisdom is that he or she can consistently strike the mean between the excesses and defects that frame each of the virtues. This is no easy task. Striking the mean depends on our emotional structures as well as on the concrete situations in which we find ourselves. At times courage will mean speaking out; at other times it will mean remaining silent. The very same dinner party that will strike us as ostentatious under one set of circumstances will strike us as generous under another set of circumstances and as niggardly under yet another set of circumstances. This is why Aristotle says that being good is a "hard job":

> It is the expert, not just anybody, who finds the center of the circle. In the same way, having a fit of temper is easy for anyone; so is giving money and spending it. But this is not so when it comes to questions of "for whom?" "how much?" "when?" "why?" and "how?" This is why goodness is rare, and is praiseworthy and fine.[5]

If what Aristotle says is correct, then policy experts would do well to develop the virtue of practical wisdom. It is not enough for policy analysts to be mere technicians, clever persons skilled in cost-effectiveness analysis, cost-benefit analysis, and risk-benefit analysis, who can find the means to any given end. Rather, they must also be wise persons, able to discern the value of the ends they pursue and able to answer the questions "for whom?" "how much?" "why?" and "how?" Likewise, it is not enough for policy analysts to be mere rhetoricians, eloquent persons schooled in the p's and q's of persuasion. Rather, they must also be virtuous persons who speak neither too much nor too little.

At this point the objection may be made that an ethics of virtue, which relies so heavily on practical wisdom, a virtue that is not perfected easily or by all, is simply too idealistic as an action guide, especially in a heterogeneous society where individuals do not agree on the worth of various ends. Supposedly, the more heterogeneous a society is, the more necessary an ethics of rules is. Unless everyone's rights, general responsibilities, and specific duties are precisely delineated, too much will be left to individual judgment, and no society bent on surviving can afford to trust its members with their own moral governance.

Although this objection gives one pause, it can be answered. Even though ancient Greece was a homogeneous society, there was considerable disagreement as to what constituted the "good for man." Some thought it was material prosperity; others thought it was power or prestige; still others thought it was the life of the mind. According to Aristotle, only the "right-minded person" could settle this dispute correctly, serving as an example for others to imitate. Imitation is not to be confused with replication, however. Given that no two individuals' moral world is alike, persons will differ as to what is the morally appropriate action for them to perform in any given situation. The power of an ideal differs from the force of a rule. It takes time to live up to an ideal, and failure to live up to it results in a sense of personal dissatisfaction. In contrast, rules are less patient. We must do what they say or be blamed for our shortcomings. Whereas rules tell us what is forbidden, permitted, or required, and threaten us with sanctions for noncompliance, ideals encourage us to put our best foot forward even when we are under no obligation to do so. This is not to suggest that, compared to laws, ideals are a weak means of "behavior control." If an ideal takes over one's life, it can effect changes that no set of rules, however clearly enunciated and strictly enforced, can ever hope to effect. However, it is to suggest that, compared to laws, ideals are noncoercive in the sense that we are free either to recognize or to ignore them as we see fit. Whereas the language of rules is that of universal similarities, the common denominator, and the father who warms his progeny that "you must, or else," the language of ideals is that of the mother who beckons her children on with the words "you can do it . . . give it a try . . . you have it in you."

If the preceding analysis is substantially correct, policy experts should be attune to the role ideals as well as moral rules play in their development as moral agents. If policy experts persist in the rote discharge of a set of rules, then they will forever remain moral infants—safe, secure, and smug in their obedience to moral laws. In contrast, if policy experts develop a moral point of view according to which moral adulthood is achieved to the degree that a person is able to live up to a set of self-imposed moral ideals, then their jobs will become a means to the kind of moral growth that produces the human analog of a giant oak rather than the human analog of a bonzai tree.

TOWARDS AN ETHICS OF VIRTUE
FOR POLICY EXPERTS: FOCUS
ON PERSONAL INTEGRITY

Although I have made no effort to hide my preference for virtue-based ethical theories in the professional realm, and although I will be speaking the language of virtues as much as possible in the next two chapters, I do not intend to renounce altogether the language of rules or to argue that virtues are a more fundamental moral phenomenon than rules. Admittedly, it would be tempting for me to argue this position, but Philippa Foot has made this task largely unnecessary. She has argued convincingly that unless a person is morally virtuous, he or she is not likely to be a dutiful follower of valid moral rules.[6] She and others have also argued that when we assess the total moral worth of a person, we do not simply focus on their discrete actions but on their unified self. We frequently make judgments like, "She's really quite nice; it's just that she flies off the handle from time to time" or "I know that he walks loudly and speaks harshly, but he's a marshmallow under that gruff exterior." And we rarely write someone off as a liar—especially if he or she is our child—on account of a few tall tales or desperate defenses ("Not me, Mom. *I* didn't do it"). Comments Tom Beauchamp:

> An overall assessment of the *person* thus depends fundamentally on whether we are confident that any given *act* exhibits the person's *character*; and even when we are certain that a person has acted wrongly on several occasions, we may still desist from judging the person's moral character until we get to know him or her better.[7]

Nevertheless, despite the persuasiveness of all the arguments made above, I do not think they are strong enough to establish the claim that virtues are a more essential moral category than principles (rules). As I see it, character and conduct go hand in hand; and a person's initial character is largely a function of parental upbringing and education. I do action x, and my parents either reward me or punish me for so doing. If I am a normal human being (amenable to the lure of pleasure and the sting of pain), rewards for x will tend to increase my type-x activities; punishments for x will tend to decrease my type-x activities. If I do action x (tell the truth) often enough, it will become part of the way I think about myself in relation to the world. Once I pride myself on being an honest person, I won't need Mom and Dad standing next to me with a sack of carrots to urge me on and a pile of sticks to rein me in. On those occasions when I do tell a lie, I will feel "out of synch" and I will ask those who know about my lie not to judge *me* on the basis of it alone. Of course, if I tell enough lies, I won't feel "out of synch." The more I repeat a certain action, the more that action becomes a part of that self I and you recognize as me.

What I wish to do in the following two chapters is to make the more modest case that although the moral universe of the policy expert can be explained by describing how the principle of utility and the categorical imperative interact within it, it can also be explained by describing the virtues policy experts must possess if they are to excel at the practice of policy analysis. Of course, it is not so easy to compile an exhaustive list of essential virtues for policy analysts. Indeed, it is not so easy to compile such a list for human beings in this society let alone for human beings in general. We noted above Aristotle's account of moral virtues[8] according to which they are settled dispositions of character that enable us to strike a balance between excess and defect in matters that affect not only our standing in the human community but also our self-image. Unlike Aristotle, contemporary ethicists are less likely to count as a moral virtue a habit that is apparently focused on the self. For the most part, contemporary ethicists operate on a definition of "moral" according to which a moral action is one that directly impinges on the well-being of people other than one's self. So, for example, it is permissible for me to be intemperate when it comes to food and drink provided that my gluttony and drunkenness neither offend other people nor affect my ability to discharge my personal and professional obligations. Even as I write this paragraph, however, it occurs to me—as it must have to Aristotle—that eating and drinking are such social activities that "closet gluttons" and "closet drunks" will be few and far between. The effects of gluttony and drunkenness can remain hidden in the private realm only so long before they manifest themselves all too visibly in the public realm. But be this as it may, it is clear that moral virtues are related both to the ways in which we see ourselves in relation to others and the ways in which others see us in relation to them. They are those traits of character, or forces internalized within us, that tend toward cohesion and community in much the same way that the vices tend toward disintegration and isolation.

By now we may be wondering whether virtues remain constant through time and across space. The virtues that hold Americans together may not be the same virtues that hold Indians together. According to Alaisdair MacIntyre, even though virtues have varied diachronically and synchronically, certain virtues appear and reappear. As he sees it, no community is possible without the virtues of justice, courage, and honesty.[9] Life would be so nasty, brutish, and short without these dispositions of character that it would simply not be worth living. Although other contemporary philosophers have added to and subtracted from MacIntyre's troika, their departures are more like variations on a common theme than new songs. For example, Peter Geach argues that the fundamental virtues are wisdom, temperance, justice, and courage;[10] G. J. Warnoch insists that they are nonmaleficence, fairness, beneficence, and nondeception;[11] Bernard Gert claims that they are truthfulness, trustworthiness, fairness, honesty, dependability, and kindness;[12] Michael Bayles suggests that they are justice, benevolence, and truthfulness;[13] and William Frankena identifies them succinctly as justice and benevolence.[14] Of all these listings, Frankena's seems most persuasive to me simply because I believe, like him, that all moral virtues can be derived either from justice or benevolence. So, for example, nonmaleficence, beneficience, and kindness are forms of benevolence; likewise, fairness, nondeception, truthfulness, trustworthiness, honesty, and dependability are aspects of justice. Any virtue that is not derivable from either justice or benevolence is probably not a moral virtue but either what Bernard Gert terms an intellectual virtue, or what I term a meta-virtue, a disposition of character like practical wisdom that facilitiates the orderly and appropriate exercise of all of a person's other virtues—be they moral or nonmoral.

If the above listing of virtues is correct, then all of us human persons—simply because we are human persons—ought to manifest the general virtues of justice and benevolence to each other. However, depending on the particular personal and professional relationships we enter into, we will also be expected to manifest certain virtues specific to them. According to Michael Bayles, professionals like doctors, lawyers, and, I would add, policy experts, will be asked to manifest the virtue of trustworthiness towards their clients. Trustworthiness, a specific moral virtue that flows from the general virtue of justice and that is further specified as including honesty, candor, competency, diligence, loyalty, and discretion (or confidentiality), is pivotal to the policy expert-policymaker relationship, because without it policymakers would be foolish to bring policy experts on board as analysts, advisers, and consultants. If you can't trust someone, there is little, if any, reason to listen to his or her observations.

In the following two chapters, we will be discussing at length the ways in which policy experts can and ought to display the specific professional virtue of trustworthiness towards their client, and the ways in which they can and ought to display the general human virtues of justice and benevolence towards so-called third parties. We will also be discussing how policy experts can and ought to handle conflicts between their obligations to their policymaking clients on the one hand, and their obligations to third parties, or the public, on the other hand. Although moral rules will usually come to the rescue in cases of conflict, unless policy experts understand the moral project as something more than the mechanical application of moral rules to life situations, they may fail to create for themselves a moral self, wise enough and imaginative enough, to sense the parameters of an ethical dilemma when rules prove to be singularly unilluminating. The more pluralistic our world becomes, the more we must rely on our moral selves to mediate the differences that threaten to tear us apart. Because unexpected moral problems are continually cropping up for which there are no ready-made rules, we must learn to trust in each other's personal integrity. "Ask Joe or ask Jane. They'll know what to do in this kind of situation. Their moral instincts are sound." Seemingly, the only alternative to focusing on our own character and that of others in morally ambiguous situations is to appeal to a law so relentless in its universality that it has no patience for the blood, sweat, and tears of us hopelessly particular human beings.

NOTES

1. Immanuel Kant, *Groundwork of the Metaphysics of Morals*, trans. H. J. Paton (New York: Harper & Row, Publishers, 1958), 74–113.

2. Alasdair MacIntyre, *After Virtue* (Notre Dame, Ind.: University of Notre Dame Press, 1981), 169–89.

3. Friedrich Nietzsche, *On the Genealogy of Morals*, ed. Walter Kaufmann (New York: Vintage Books, 1969), 24–56.

4. A. E. Taylor, trans. *Aristotle* (New York: Dover Publications, Inc., 1955), 91.

5. Aristotle, *Nicomachean Ethics*, bk. 2, ch. 7, trans. A. E. Wardman, in *The Philosophy of Aristotle* ed. Renford Bambrough (New York: Mentor Books, 1963).

6. Philippa Foot, *Virtues and Vices* (Oxford, England: Basil Blackwell, 1978), 12-14.

7. Tom L. Beauchamp, *Philosophical Ethics* (New York: McGraw-Hill Book Company, 1982), 165.

8. According to Aristotle, there are intellectual virtues as well as moral virtues.

9. MacIntyre, *After Virtue*, 178.

10. Peter Geach, *The Virtues: The Stanton Lectures 1973-4* (Cambridge, England: Cambridge University Press, 1977).

11. G. J. Warnoch, *The Object of Morality* (London: Methuen & Co., Ltd., London, 1971).

12. Bernard Gert, *The Moral Rules* (New York: Harper & Row, Publishers, Inc., 1970).

13. Michael Bayles, *Professional Ethics* (Belmont, California: Wadsworth Publishing Company, 1981), 70-85.

14. William Frankena, *Ethics* (Englewood Cliffs, N.J.: Prentice-Hall, Inc., 1963), 42.

Chapter 6

The Policy Expert's Obligation
to the Policymaking Client

The key ethical issue for any profession or occupation is whether its members are governed by special moral principles and rules that are different from, or even in conflict with, the common moral framework. Many doctors assume that the principles embedded in the Hippocratic oath mean that their sole duty is to the patient's health, even if that means deceiving their patients; and many lawyers believe that the principle of full advocacy gives them license to trample third parties' rights in order to promote their clients' interests. Business executives sometimes claim that consumers' rights may be sacrificed in the name of stockholders' profits; and politicians oftentimes argue that their office requires them to dirty their hands for the sake of the common good.

As we noted in Chapter 4, Alan H. Goldman among others has argued against this schizophrenic moral view.[1] Increasingly, the dominant point of view seems to be that the same ethics govern both our private and professional lives. Policy experts do not have two moral hats, one to wear to the office and the other to wear at home. Rather, they must make do with one moral hat for all occasions, public or private. This is not to suggest, however, that the role of policy expert is ethically identical with, say, the role of father or mother. Depending on what part they play in the policymaking process, policy analysts and advisers will be required either to exhibit virtues that they need not routinely exercise as parents or to exhibit homey virtues in extraordinary ways.

Policy experts' virtues differ from those of parents and of other professionals because policy analysis is a practice readily distinguishable both from parenting and from other professional activities like business, medicine, and law. The virtues policy experts are expected to exhibit and the corresponding principles they are expected to follow flow from their relationship to their policymaking clients. Since the central issue in articulating any professional-client relationship (doctor-patient, lawyer-client, teacher-student) is the allocation of responsibility and authority in decision making, what we are looking for in the next few pages is an appropriate moral model to guide this allocation insofar as policy experts and policymakers are concerned.

THE PROFESSIONAL-CLIENT RELATIONSHIP

Michael Bayles has presented five models for the professional-client relationship in general: agency, contract, friendship, paternalism, and fiduciary. Each of these models is predicated upon a different understanding of the authority/responsibility calculus. According to Bayles, all these models, with the exception of the fifth, are ethically flawed. Only the fiduciary model correctly represents the proper form for the professional-client relationship.[2]

The Agency Model

As applied to the policy expert-policymaker relationship, the agency model assumes that because a client (usually a policymaker) either has sufficient knowledge to direct analysts and advisers or sufficient power to control them, they are simply the client's agents. That such a relationship frequently exists in the policy arena is a well-documented fact. Examples abound of policy experts who play the role of agent. When Eisenhower appointed Dr. James Killian, president of MIT, as Special Assistant for Science and Technology, there was little debate over the functions of the new science adviser other than disappointment in some quarters that the special assistant had no powers of command or control. Killian was not anointed "missile czar."[3] His role was simply to mobilize the best scientific brain power in the country behind a President who was straining to discharge his obligations as the head of an enormous peacetime bureaucracy. Nonetheless, because he realized how much help he needed to rule wisely, when Eisenhower referred to members of the newly constituted President's Science Advisory Committee (PSAC) as "my scientists," there was always a tone of pride rather than possession in his voice.

With the exception of John Fitzgerald Kennedy, presidents subsequent to Eisenhower treated policy experts with less esteem, tending to reduce them to mere administration mouthpieces or hired brains. When Lyndon B. Johnson took over after J.F.K.'s assassination, Jerome Wiesner, who had served as Kennedy's science adviser, realized that he would have to leave the White House shortly: "I've been on Johnson's wrong side too often," commented Wiesner.[4] And when Nixon was elected, the PSAC sensed that its days were numbered. Insisting that *his* scientists should routinely effect Copernican revolutions in which their data were made to fit his world views rather than vice versa, Nixon had no use for uncooperative devil's advocates. On the contrary, he made it perfectly clear that two principles alone should govern a presidential adviser's conduct: (1) Judge not the President's ends, lest ye be judged; and (2) work assiduously to advance those ends. Comments one former high-ranking science adviser:

If a Science Adviser is going to count, he must be a foot-soldier marching to the program of the President, not the company chaplain. The Science Adviser is recruited into a policy management system that is committed to a political agenda. His job, basically, is to use his wits and expertise to inform the choices of a President and to carry his share of the President's burden. . . . He can do this in a straightforward way as long as he is seen to be supporting the main directions of the administration and not obstructing them. It is not a clear line of sight, and it is not unheard of for a willful President or one of his purely political henchmen to grind his teeth over the conscientious staff advice he is given, and to murmur, "Who will rid me of this troublesome priest?"[5]

Seemingly, on this account, the best science adviser is the one who serves as an obliging data bank programmed to flow where his or her President's political fortunes blow; and *certeris paribus*, the best policy expert is the one who simply does as he or she is told. But such science advisers and policy experts resemble too closely the "expert witness for hire," who, for an agreed-upon fee, will testify as willingly for the prosecution as for the defense in a criminal case, and it is simply not clear that those in the know ought to sell their services unquestioningly to the highest bidder in power.

The Paternalism Model

Whereas the agency model reduces the policy adviser or analyst to instrumental status, the paternalism model threatens a similar reduction with respect to the policymaking client. With rare exceptions, few policymakers have either the experts' knowledge and skills or experience and insights. Therefore, or so the argument goes, let those in the know, the policy advisers and analysts, have primary authority and responsibility for decisionmaking.

Depending on how much respect one has for science and technology, the above argument has more or less initial plausibility. Before WW II, for example, scientists were usually characterized as absent-minded professors, completely ignorant of the world and inexperienced in its ways. Immediately after WW II, however, when the discoveries that led to Hiroshima were fully publicized, scientists were regarded as the ultimate authorities on all possible subjects. As we noted in Chapter 3, it seemed for a moment as if the philosopher-king had been incarnated in the guise of physicist.[6] This American love affair with physicists in particular and with scientists in general reached its zenith during the Kennedy administration. John F. Kennedy flooded the White House with the best and the brightest. These "whiz kids" were favored by the Chief Executive, and no meeting of any import could be called without a cadre of them in attendance.

Although administrations subsequent to Kennedy's continued to rely on experts for analysis and advice, they did so somewhat grudgingly; and by the late 1970s this nation's brains had fallen from political grace. Currently many Americans are of the opinion that experts must be put in their place lest public policy become the captive of a scientific-technological elite. Comments Solly Zucherman, himself a scientist and adviser,

Harold Macmillan once observed that politicians have to run hard to catch up with the scientists. But if their goal is peace, then politicians are in the wrong race. . . . In the twenty years since the first major effort was made to bring the nuclear arms race to an end, masses of water have flowed under the bridge. If the bridge itself is not to become submerged, the politicians will have to take charge of the technical men.[7]

Certainly this is easier said than done. But in a democracy it must be done, for the people have entrusted their decision-making powers to those men and women who profess to share their fundamental values, whether or not these persons can grasp the subtleties of economics, physics, chemistry, and so on. The people expect policymakers to secure the assistance of advisers and analysts, but they do not expect policymakers to cede their decision-making powers to expets who, after all, did not campaign for office.

The Friendship Model

The next two related models, the friendship and contract models, represent an advance over both the agency and the paternalism models in that neither the policy expert nor the policymaker is reduced to instrumental status; both are viewed as equals, coresponsible for the results of their policy deliberations. According to the friendship model, policy advisers and analysts should have a close relationship of mutual trust and cooperation with policymakers. They should view each other as partners involved in a mutual venture. Referring explicitly to presidential advising, Isidor Rabi, chairman of the original PSAC, insists that

For an optimal relationship, the Science Adviser must know and understand the problems of the President as he sees them, as they exist in government. Therefore he has to be close to the President, see him frequently, see his aides frequently, so that he fully comprehends what the situation- is and does not offer irrelevant advice or, worse yet, advice based on misunderstanding the situation. He must be a person who will like the President in the sense of really wishing him well and wishing to help him and wishing to subordinate his own preferences, political or societal, to the needs of the President for the policy which comes naturally to him. All this means that the Science Adviser must try to be a part of the President's mind-set.[8]

But even if policy experts *could* become part of policymakers' brains, *should* they? Not if they turn out to be mere yea-sayers, imbued with the spirit of Lord Brougham, the nineteenth-century advocate who argued that

An advocate, in the discharge of his duty, knows but one person in all the world, and that person is his client. To save that client by all means and expedients, and at all hazards and costs to other persons, and, amongst them, to himself, is his first and only duty; and in performing this duty he must not regard the alarm, the torments, the destruction which he may bring upon others.[9]

In sum, the problem with the friendship model is that it is predicated upon the assumption that friends are permitted, even required, not only to take each others' interests seriously, but also to give them more weight than those of other persons. Thus, experts should look out for policymakers' interests, agreeing to legitimate their policies. In return, policymakers should look out for experts' interests, assuring them a place in the sun. This is all well and good provided that the public does not suffer by virtue of their exclusion from this symbiotic support system. If, as an ordinary citizen who represents nobody's interests but her own, I am not entitled to violate your rights simply because I am friends with someone else, then as an elected policymaker who does represent the interests of her entire constituency, I may not even deny you some benefit, let alone do you some harm, in order to secure an equivalent benefit or to avoid an equivalent harm for a personal or professional friend. Indeed, *in my role of elected policymaker*, I should either remain friendless or be friends with each and every citizen. Any other course of action verges on a favoritism antithetical to the democratic ethos.

The Contract Model

The contract model is an improvement over the friendship model for several reasons. It preserves what was good about the friendship model—the notion of equality—while avoiding what was bad about it—the spirit of "cronyism." Nonetheless, the contract model fails because a policy expert and a policymaker can no more contract to an equal distribution of decision-making powers than a man and a woman can contract to a polygamous or bigamous marriage. Such contracts are null and void. The only decision-making powers policymakers may assuredly delegate to policy experts are those confined to the realm of the purely technical or merely mechanical; and that realm is, as we have seen, quite constricted, if not nonexistent. When it comes to questions of value, however, the situation is otherwise. Although it is difficult to separate facts from values, policymakers need to see whose values are operative at each stage of the policy process. The people's? Their own personal values? The experts'? In particular, policymakers must probe their analysts' and advisers' recommendations. As we noted in Chapter 2, many of these recommendations involve nontechnical assumptions or judgments in varying degrees. In some cases the policymakers themselves supply the nontechnical assumptions, but more often than not they are at least partly supplied by the advisers and analysts. For instance, in the judgment as to the safety of a nuclear reactor installation, "safety" is a relative term. In a sense, the only truly safe reactor is the one that is never built. Every technical judgment on safety is actually a subtle balancing of risk against opportunity, of cost against benefit—the risk or cost of injury to the public against the possible or actual benefits of nuclear power. Much of the apparent disagreement among scientists about nuclear energy stems not from a conflict as to actual technical facts, but rather from a difference of views as to the relative weight to be assigned identifiable risks, costs, opportunities, and benefits. Policymakers have to be careful not to accept advisers' and analysts' judgments at face value; for the people have entrusted them, and not the experts, to weigh variables in a way they themselves would weigh them. Policymakers may, from time to time, wish to rid themselves of this responsibility, but it is the burden which goes with the privileges of office.

The Fiduciary Model

Although we seem to have exhausted all possible models for the relationship that should exist between policy experts and policymakers, one remains—the so-called fiduciary model used by Michael Bayles to clarify the doctor-patient and lawyer-client relationships. By virtue of their superior knowledge, doctors and lawyers assume special obligations toward their patients and clients respectively. Unlike doctors, patients do not know how to treat cancer, and so they depend on doctors to outline their treatment options; and unlike lawyers, clients do not know how to plead a case, and so they rely on lawyers to suggest courtroom strategies. Nonetheless, because it is the patient's health or life at stake, it is he who must decide whether to have chemotherapy or not. Similarly, because it is the defendant's property, freedom, or even life at stake, it is she who must decide whether to plea bargain or not. It is neither the right nor the duty of doctors or lawyers to make such crucial decisions for patients or clients, provided, of course, that the latter are competent adults.

Admittedly, this model does not precisely fit the relationship between a policy expert and a policymaker. Unlike patients or clients, policymakers do not act on their own behalf but on behalf of the people they represent. And unlike doctors or lawyers, advisers and analysts are serving not so much, if at all, the policymaker's personal interests as their agency's or department's interests. In other words, experts serve not so much the man or the woman who has assumed public office as the office itself. Nonetheless, the fiduciary model captures what is essential about the relationship between policy experts and policymakers in a democratic society. It recognizes the superior knowledge that experts have and imposes special obligations upon them in virtue of their superior knowledge, yet it insists that it is the clients, the policymakers, who have ultimate decision-making power. Policymakers must rely on policy experts to analyze problems, formulate alternative courses of action, determine the likely consequences of the alternatives, make recommendations, and use their expertise in helping them carry out their decisions. Because policymakers depend on policy experts, policy experts must be worthy of their clients' trust in performing these tasks. In turn, policy analysts and advisers expect their policymaker clients to preserve the integrity of their work and to use it for agreed-upon purposes. Because experts entrust their policymaker clients with the fruits of their intellect, policymakers betray them whenever they misuse, abuse, distort, or pad their studies.

THE VIRTUES OF THE POLICY EXPERT

In his study of professional ethics, Michael Bayles suggests that there are at least six specific virtues that a trustworthy professional must exhibit toward his or her client. These virtues are honesty, candor, competence, diligence, loyalty, and discretion.

Although this list of virtues is, as Bayles himself admits, probably neither exhaustive nor mutually exclusive,[10] it is a good working list which permits us to articulate the policy expert-policymaker relationship in a productive way.

Honesty and Candor

Bayles draws several distinctions between dishonesty and candor that are more or less compelling. As he sees it, the dishonest person uses others' trust of him to get into a position where he can violate that trust in a way that advances his own selfish purposes. Thus, for example, a conniving policy expert who knows as much about health care as about the mating habits of Inner Mongolian moths can, if he is wily enough, worm himself into the President's heart and be appointed the head of a very well paying commission on health care. The person who lacks candor, on the other hand, is not necessarily selfish. According to Bayles, such a person is as likely to tell falsehoods intentionally and/or to withhold true information knowingly for altruistic as for selfish reasons.[11] Thus, in *The Sting*, those two charming conmen, Paul Newman and Robert Redford, who used every trick in the books to help out an establishment that had been ruthlessly victimized by the mob, lacked candor rather than honesty.

Although it is not clear how much is gained by these fine-grained distinctions between honesty and candor, it is clear that policy experts who act less than honestly and candidly violate policymakers' trust. Assume, for example, that a policymaker hires three policy analysts to provide independent evaluations of a welfare program akin to the Head Start program. The innovative educational program has two sets of goals: (1) to improve the cognitive and affective skills of underprivileged preschoolers so that they can compete effectively with more privileged children by the time they reach school age; and (2) to improve the health and nutrition standards of the communities from which the underprivileged children come. Unbeknownst to the policymaker, policy analyst #1 is adamantly opposed to welfare in any form; policy analyst #2 is totally amenable to welfare in any form; and policy analyst #3 is neutral—well, as neutral as they come. Eager to prove that the preschool program is not worth hefty government expenditures, policy analyst #1 first engages in a little posturing, masquerading as an objective analyst when he is in fact a very biased one. Having created a false impression, analyst #1 then proceeds to submarine the program. He torpedoes it by ignoring the strides it has made in the area of improved health and nutrition standards and by focusing on its shortcomings in the area of children's cognitive and affective development. In contrast, analyst #2, who is eager to vindicate the innovative program for underprivileged tots, also engages in some preliminary posturing—"I'm the objective one, not policy analyst #1"—before exhibiting his talents both for eyewashing (the attempt to justify a weak program by deliberately selecting for evaluation only those aspects that look good on the surface) and for whitewashing (the attempt to cover up program failure or error by avoiding any objective appraisal).[12] By dint of concerted effort, analyst #2 manages to reveal the program's strengths and to conceal its weaknesses. In contrast to analysts #1 and #2, analyst #3 "tells it like it is" with a view to exposing both the strengths and weaknesses of the program. A totally honest person, analyst #3 warns her client that, try as she might to remain objective, some of her "bleeding-heart" biases are likely to filter through the lines of her report. Indeed, so great is her desire to be candid that analyst #3 is particularly careful to write reports that are as far from obfuscation—the attempt to camouflage what has been observed through the maximum use of unintelligible jargon—as possible. As a result, analyst #3 alone provides the policymaker with the kind of information he or she needs to forge enlightened public policy.

Although it would seem as if honesty and candor are virtues that are framed on the one side by their corresponding defects of dishonesty and blanket untruthfulness, it is not immediately clear that they are framed on the other side by corresponding excesses. Can someone be too honest or too candid, or are these virtues ones that admit of no excess? If ordinary language is any guide here, then it is possible to be too honest and/or too candid. Anyone who has worked through a volatile issue with a group of people knows that totally exposing one's views immediately is usually disastrous. Admit at the first meeting of the committee on educational policy that you are an egalitarian who is unequivocally opposed to Phi Beta Kappa and all the elitists on the committee will forthwith label you "a mediocre mind" and dismiss everything you ever say until the day you retire. Play it cool, however, and eke out your beliefs one by one, and you will have a greater chance of persuading some of the elitists some of the time of at least some of your egalitarian ideas. Thus, policy experts do have to be sensitive to problems of timing and style, especially when there is reason to believe that the policymaker is likely to reject an excellent analysis simply because the experts came on too quickly or too strongly. Similarly, anyone who has ever received a report longer than 10 pages with more than three suggested courses of action highlighted in the addendum knows that too much information can be as great a liability as too little information. Overwhelmed by pounds of paperwork and presented with scores of options, the policymaker may throw up his hands in despair and flip a coin. Thus, in her desire to be honest and candid, the policy expert must not fall prey to the notion that a longer analysis is necessarily a better one. Swamping a policymaker with a morass of unnecessary details may do more to cloud than to enlighten matters.

On occasion, lack of honesty and candor may be a morally excusable—if not also justifiable—course of action.[13] In his article, "Temptations and Risks of the Scientific Adviser," R. V. Jones points out that

> A moral problem can arise when an analyst believes that he is a better judge of the course to be followed than the man or men who have to take the final decision. If he gives completely open evidence, he may risk their taking the opposite course, and occasionally the consequences could be so serious that he may ask himself whether or not he ought to put the facts completely openly, especially if he alone has discovered a fact which will go against his argument, and yet which he does not believe to be crucial.[14]

Jones cites as an example of such a moral problem the development of radar in Britain during the Second World War. New additions to the radar team quickly discovered that the "old hands" were so committed to making radar work that it simply "was 'not done' to suggest that the whole affair would not work."[15] Despite the fact that around 1937 some members of the radar team suspected that radar was vulnerable to simple electronic countermeasures, like the dropping of aluminum foil strips to "confuse" radar screens, they did not report their suspicions to the Royal Air Force lest it withdraw support from their research. Largely because the RAF remained unaware of radar's flaws, it continued to pour funds into the so-called Bawdsey project. Radar was developed, and thanks to it the crucial Battle of Britain was won. Therefore, or so the consequentialist concludes, withholding the nasty facts about aluminum was justified. The end—Britain's deliverance—certainly justified the means: temporarily withholding some confusing information from the RAF.

What is problematic about this consequentialist rationale for withholding information, however, is that the consequences could easily have been otherwise. What if the Germans had found out about the amazing properties of aluminum foil and developed countermeasures to radar before the Battle of Britain? The British radar system would then have been defenseless against German planes precisely because the countermeasure problem had been squelched in 1937.[16] Nevertheless, there may be nonconsequentialist justifications for what amounted to a paternalistic decision on the part of the radar experts, who speculated that the RAF would panic unnecessarily at the first hint of a possible defect in a basically sound system of antiaircraft defense.

Whenever paternalism is justified, it tends to be justified on one of the following grounds, neatly summarized by Michael Bayles in his *Professional Ethics*:

1. The agent has superior knowledge as to what is in a person's best interest. Because the agent knows better than the person what is best, the agent is justified in acting to avoid significant harm to, or procure a significant benefit for, the person. . . .

2. The client is incapable of giving a fully free and informed consent. By "fully free" is meant without duress, psychological compulsion, or other emotional or psychological disturbance. By "informed" is meant with appreciation of the consequences of a course of conduct and its alternatives. If people cannot give such consent, then their decisions will not adequately reflect their reasonable desires and will not be expressions of their "true selves." . . .

3. A person will later come to agree that the decision was correct. Although the person does not now consent, he will later.[17]

Assuming that the officials of the RAF were capable of making a fully free and informed decision about whether to continue or to discontinue the funding of radar research—a reasonable enough assumption—we will be able to justify the radar experts' tight-lipped policy only if either criterion 1 or 3, above, is met. Either we will argue that because superior knowledge always trumps superior power, the radar scientists' expertise *ex hypothesi* overrode the RAF's interest in making its own decisions—right or wrong. Or we will argue that even though the RAF would have decided to terminate the funding of radar in 1937 had the experts told all, it would have thanked its lucky stars after the Battle of Britain that the experts chose to keep quiet, thus serving both the RAF's and Britain's best interests.

The problem with the second leg of this either-or justification is that its strength rests too heavily on the fact that the Battle of Britain was won.[18] Had this crucial battle been lost because of failed radar, my guess is that the RAF would have condemned rather than praised the radar experts for their "brains know best" stance. Nevertheless, in the absence of other alternatives, to the degree that those in the know are as certain as they can be that a significant harm, to which those in power have publicly declared opposition, will in fact occur if those in power are given the right information at the wrong time, then, to that same degree, policy experts are justified in temporarily withholding information from their policymaking clients. So great is our respect both for individual autonomy and for representative government, however, that we are unlikely to justify any more aggressively paternalistic step than this one. Policy experts may appeal to their superior knowledge to justify their lack of total honesty or candor, but they may do so only when the interests they profess to serve have been identified, in some *public* way, as the actual interests of their policymaking clients, which, presumably, are the interests of the people at large. Second-guessing someone's interests is simply not permitted in a society where the substitution of X's interests for those of Y frequently masquerades as paternalism.

The Virtues of Competence and Diligence

Like honesty and candor, competence and diligence are Siamese twins resistant to conceptual separation. Suffice it to say, however, that a policy expert can be exceptionally competent but not noticeably diligent, or noticeably diligent but exceptionally incompetent.[19] For example, a competent policy expert, well trained in his particular area of expertise and incredibly skilled in the general techniques of policy analysis, may nonetheless fail to produce valuable reports as a result of his sheer laziness. Similarly, a diligent policy expert, who always tries to do her best to go the extra mile, may be unable to write a sound analysis simply because she lacks the talent and/or the necessary skills to do so.

A responsibility of competence clearly follows from the rule that a policy expert must be worthy of a policymaker's trust. "Faking it" and "bluffing one's way through" are unacceptable behavior patterns for the policy expert. Policymakers hire experts on the assumption that the experts can provide them with a service no one else can provide or provide as well. If the "expert" is not really an expert—if he or she does not have the wherewithal to perform certain tasks—then the "expert" is a fraud. Unfortunately, it is not always clear whether a policy expert is or is not qualified to perform a certain task. Although policy experts have an obligation not to get in over their heads, they also have an obligation to excel in their chosen occupation. If policy experts are to develop their skills, however, then they must attempt challenging tasks from time to time. Imagine a pianist who never played a piece more difficult than the one he or she had currently mastered. The concert hall would be full of men in tuxedoes and women in gowns playing chopsticks! Although a staff economist for the Department of Defense, for example, may know next to nothing about welfare, she can often learn enough about it to produce a first-rate analysis. For the most part, the policy expert's skills are transferrable. Once an economist has mastered the basic techniques of policy analysis, she can as easily work for the head of social services as for a military general.

Like the virtue of competence, the virtue of diligence also follows from the ground virtue of trustworthiness. Diligence is the requirement that an analyst work carefully and promptly, though not hastily. In the realm of policy analysis, there is pressure to speed things up—but since haste can spell not only waste but also disaster, the analyst must resist such pressure when standards of care dictate that he move more deliberately.

Once again, there is something paternalistic about the expert's stand here. In essence, the analyst is telling the policymaker that the policymaker does not know how long it takes to produce a good study, and that it is in the policymaker's best interest not to hound his or her staff of experts. On the assumption that policymakers do in fact want the best as opposed to the quickest report, this weakly paternalistic action is probably strongly justified. Of course, there is a mean between a very quick and dirty report and an extremely slow and clean report. If the defect of diligence is best articulated as slipshoddiness, then its excess is probably best conceived as anal-attentiveness to every detail of a task.

In addition to devoting neither too little nor too much time to any given task, the diligent expert has a second-order task to make sure that he or she has adequate time to discharge his or her duties well. Policy experts should undertake only as many tasks as they can do well, resisting the temptation to be lauded as the department's, bureau's, or office's go-getter. Laziness is no virtue, but neither is taking on more than one can handle.

The Virtues of Loyalty and Discretion

Far more problematic than the virtues of honesty, candor, competence, and diligence are the virtues of loyalty and discretion. Rarely do experts exhibit the former virtues in excess. In contrast, experts are prone to be overly loyal and discreet. There is a natural tendency to stand by an employer, especially if that employer is either a very powerful person or a very generous person to whom debts of gratitude are owed.

Since professionals are hired by their clients to perform tasks for them, it is true that policy experts must be loyal to their policymaking clients. If an employer cannot trust his employees, then that employer is in for trouble. But loyalty has its limits. A professional's loyalty can be affected by conflicts of interest between the client and himself/herself or between the client and third parties. Thus honesty demands that policy experts, for example, reveal such conflicts to their policymaking clients even though such revelations may signal transfers, demotions, or nasty falls from grace for the experts.

Admittedly, it is quite difficult for professionals to walk the tightrope between loyalty and honesty. As we noted in Chapter 4, bureaucracies thrive on loyal subjects, and anyone who works in a bureaucratic context long enough will be subject to the blandishments of the institutional ethos. If the expert is not perceived as a team player, then "his phone will seldom ring, he will have a tough time forcing his way into the first circle of decision analysis, and he will eat lonely meals in the White House mess."[20] Policy experts who fail to play ball with policymakers will not be given important work to do. But this suggests that the price of effectiveness or success as an adviser is independence of judgment. Some analysts and advisers deny this, insisting that loyal experts are permitted to speak their minds. Depending on the openness of the policymaker, this may be the case; but recent history indicates that many a spirited policy expert has shriveled in the presence of an opinionated policymaker. For example, during the Vietnam years, several of President Johnson's analytic staff disagreed with his policies, and yet their dissent was diluted. Chester Cooper describes his domestication as follows:

> During the process I would frequently fall into a Walter-Mitty-like fantasy: when my turn came I would rise to my feet slowly, look around the room and then directly look at the President and say, very quietly and emphatically, "Mr. President, gentlemen, I most definitely do *not* agree." But I was removed from my trance when I heard the President's voice saying, "Mr. Copper, do you agree?" And out would come a "Yes, Mr. President, I agree."[21]

Discretion, a virtue closely connected to loyalty, rests upon the clients' value of privacy in not having information about them or their activities conveyed to others without their consent. Like loyalty, however, discretion also has its limits. For example, what should a policy analyst do if he knows that his or her policymaking client is engaged in activities that betray the public trust? The analyst can keep quiet and be loyal to his client but disloyal to the public at large; he can go to the client and threaten disclosure, in which case he will be viewed as disloyal and will have no future in the policy arena; or he can quit and look for another job in which to fight the good fight. But if the analyst is a fairly senior expert, there may not be a job open to him in the bureaucracy. The last places of retreat are the think tanks and universities. Unfortunately, these ivory towers are beginning to resemble government and corporate hierarchies. Since it is difficult to be appropriately loyal and discreet under such circumstances, it is increasingly important to articulate the ethical principles that govern resignation, whistleblowing, and leaking—a task to which the next chapter on the policy experts' obligations to third parties is devoted. For now, suffice it to say that of all the virtues in the policy experts' repertoire, none are more difficult to exhibit without excess or deficiency than the virtues of loyalty and discretion.

THE PERILS OF PARTISAN ADVOCACY

One of the questions that we can no longer skirt is whether, in the execution of their duties, policy experts can serve as partisan advocates. Given all that we said in Chapter 2, it is clear that no policy expert is capable of total neutrality and objectivity. Thus, when we ask whether the policy expert is permitted to act as a partisan advocate, we are asking whether that expert is permitted to use strategies on behalf of his or her policymaking clients' interests analogous to those a lawyer uses on behalf of his or her client's interests.

Recently, this question has been raised forcefully by the Operations Research Society of America. Operations research was first used extensively by the United States Department of Defense during World War II. Initially concerned with evaluating the relative cost and effectiveness of various radar systems, American and British scientists gradually extended their statistical methods to the analysis of aerial bombing raids, the evaluation of weapons and equipment, and to the analysis of specific tactical operations. After the war, the techniques of operations research were applied to the direction and management of large systems of men, machines, materials, and money in industry and government. So successful were these applications that operations research remains one of the most widely used techniques of policy analysis.[22] Wed as they are to numbers, operations researchers are, by instinct, positivists committed to the objectivity and neutrality of numbers. Nevertheless, as a result of several controversial cases, an increasing number of operations researchers are less convinced that numbers never lie and more convinced that a quantitative report is only as value-free as the operations researcher who produces it.

The ABM Controversy

One of the episodes that has most contributed to this self-doubt on the part of operations researchers is the 1969 debate before the Senate Armed Services Committee on the Safeguard ABM (antiballistic missile) defense system for American Minuteman missiles. The two main protagonists were Professor George Rathjens, who opposed the need for an ABM defense system, and Professor Albert Wohlstetter, who testified in its favor. The intensity of the debate between Rathjens and Wohlstetter resulted in a heated exchange of letters in *The New York Times*, an investigation by the Operations Research Society of America, and the subsequent publication of a set of guidelines for operations researchers.

In his statement before the Armed Services Committee, Rathjens raised two questions: (1) Are our strategic retaliatory forces likely to be dangerously vulnerable to preemptive attack in the near future? and (2) if so, is the deployment of antiballistic missiles the best way to handle this type of weakness? Setting himself in opposition to the administration, Rathjens roared "no" to both these questions. In Rathjen's opinion, the $2.1 billion cost of building an ABM system was not worth the strain on the American budget since, *even in the unlikelihood that a reasonably effective system could be perfected*, nothing crucial in the way of either defense or offense would be gained. Observed Rathjens:

> Even if the Soviet SS-9 missile force were to grow as rapidly as the Defense Department's most worrisome projections, even if the Soviet Union were to develop and employ MIRVs [Multiple Independently Targetable Reentry Vehicles] with those missiles and even if they achieved accuracies as good as we

apparently expect with our MIRV forces . . . , a quarter of our Minuteman force could be expected to survive a Soviet preemptive SS-9 attack. That quarter alone would be more than enough to inflict unacceptable damage on the U.S.S.R.[23]

Upon hearing Rathjen's estimates, Dr. Wohlstetter, his opponent, was distressed. His calculations showed that no more than 5 percent of our Minuteman missiles could withstand a Soviet preemptive onslaught. Wohlstetter insisted that Rathjens's numbers were off because three of Rathjen's basic assumptions were faulty. According to Wohlstetter, Rathjens had (1) overestimated the blast resistance for Minuteman silos by two thirds, (2) underestimated the Russian bomb yield per SS-9 by approximately 11 megatons, and (3) severely underestimated the Russians' ability to make good use of partial information on our missile malfunctions.[24]

Angered by Wohlstetter's attack, Rathjens wrote to *The New York Times*, which had published an article about the Rathjens-Wohlstetter debate. In this letter Rathjens argued that not his but Wohlstetter's analysis was faulty. He also revealed his desire to limit the nuclear arms race:

> The most effective means of insuring the continued viability of the Minuteman force is early agreement to stop MIRV testing and to preclude a large build-up in Soviet ICBM strength. Negotiations to achieve these ends clearly merit higher priority than the deployment of Safeguard.[25]

In a heated rejoinder to *The Times*, Wohlstetter accused Rathjens of naive politics as well as sloppy science. The Soviets, warned Wohlstetter, are not to be trusted. Military agreements with the U.S. notwithstanding, the U.S.S.R. has every intention of first attaining and then maintaining nuclear arms superiority. Following Wohlstetter's virulent attack, in yet another *Times* letter, Rathjens accused his opponent of misrepresenting him. To this charge Wohlstetter replied, in a final newspaper letter, that if anyone was at fault it was Rathjens, who had propagated low-quality analysis, glibly invoking the "authority of science" without employing its meticulous methods.[26]

Concerned that operations researchers were being discredited in the public eye for failure to produce uncontestable facts, the Operations Research Society of America decided to adjudicate the Rathjens/Wohlstetter exchange. In the course of its investigation, ORSA found that Rathjens and other anti-ABM experts had presented "inappropriate," "misleading," and even "factually erroneous" material about Safeguard deployment.[27] Although ORSA did not give the pro-ABM scientists an entirely clean bill of health, it implied that the pro-ABM scientists' faults were mere pecadilloes compared to the grievous omissions and commissions of the anti-ABM scientists. ORSA claimed that the anti-ABM scientists' failure to distinguish properly between the roles of analyst (assessor of facts) and advocate (espouser of values) had inspired their shoddy research. In particular, ORSA singled out Rathjens for criticism. Supposedly, he had abused the principles of sound analysis in ten respects:

1. Failure to present assumptions and facilitate the constructive discussion of differences among experts.
2. Improper use of source material.
3. Failure to incorporate major features of systems under consideration.
4. Use of inefficient tactics and failure to look at a suitable range of strategies.
5. Suggestions of impractical alternatives.
6. Use of improper criteria.
7. Use of improper costing.
8. Failure to recognize the multifunctional character of systems.
9. Failure to recognize lead-time systems.
10. Failure to address the potential system interactions.[28]

ORSA concluded its critique of Rathjens by castigating scientists who behave like passionate *advocates*, obscuring the weaknesses of their positions and putting forth "unsupported allegations," and by praising scientists who behave like dispassionate *analysts*, restricting themselves to the quantifiable and logically structured aspects of problems.[29]

Embedded in ORSA's report was the suggestion that Rathjens, for political and perhaps moral reasons, deliberately introduced misinformation and distortion into his data ·to produce an unwarranted conclusion (no ABM system). What ORSA failed to consider, argues critic Paul Doty, were two other possibilities: (1) that a large measure of "bias" flows from "honest conviction" rather than the "attempt to deceive"; and (2) that a large measure of "bias" is simply ineliminatable, since scientists are unable to escape all the scientific theories, political commitments, and ethical ideals that mold their perceptions of the facts.[30]

In his thoughtful assessment of ORSA's report, Doty points out that the Senate asked the experts before it three questions: (1) Given that we have an excellent supply of air-based missiles (bombers) and sea-based missiles (submarines), just *how necessary* is the protection of some or all of our land-based missiles? (2) Assuming that our land-based missiles are necessary for our defense, does Safeguard provide the *most adequate* (possible and feasible) protection for them? (3) Leaving aside questions of necessity and adequacy, do we net a *political advantage* by building a Safeguard system?[31] Whereas the pro-ABM scientists concentrated on questions of necessity, notes Doty, the anti-ABM scientists focused on questions of adequacy. Curiously, however, the ORSA review committee did not divide its time equally between questions of necessity and adequacy. Rather, it chose to focus on questions of *necessity*, faulting the anti-ABM scientists for spending too much time on questions of adequacy and not enough time on questions of necessity. Had the review committee focused on questions of *adequacy* instead, it might have concluded that not the anti-ABM scientists but the pro-ABM scientists were remiss. Given ORSA's decision to focus on questions of necessity, however, the cynic is prone to speculate that ORSA favored the pro-ABM scientists either because it preferred Wohlstetter's brand of science or because it preferred Wohlstetter's political leanings. But even if cynicism about ORSA's motives is not called for, skepticism about its powers of judgment is in order. ORSA failed to notice how Wohlstetter's unexamined and unargued attribution of maximum nuclear capability to America prompted him not only to exaggerate the need for Safeguard, but also to overestimate its adequacy as a line of defense and its usefulness as a political weapon. *If* ORSA was right to question Rathjens's values, it was wrong not to challenge Wohlstetter's.

Morale of the ABM Controversy

What is most instructive about ORSA's investigation, other than the fact that professional organizations can be as biased as the persons it seeks to censor, is the fact that policy experts are troubled by the concept of policy advocacy. Without providing convincing arguments. ORSA simply announced that operations researchers ought to avoid advocacy at all costs. There are, however, arguments that support policy advocacy as well as arguments that oppose it.

Those who favor policy advocacy often draw analogies between the professional role of policy experts and that of lawyers. In a criminal trial, the prosecution constructs the strongest case against the defendant, while the defense does just the opposite. Because both the prosecutor and the defense counsel act as partisans, they supposedly get the strongest arguments and most accurate criticism out on the table. Once these arguments are articulated, the strongest side supposedly wins the day. Thus truth emerges. The innocent go home free and the guilty are imprisoned. But, continue the proponents of policy advocacy, if the adversary process serves truth so well in the legal realm, then it will probably serve truth equally well in the policy world. Experts who support a policy ought to engage in a heated debate with those experts who oppose it. As soon as the pros and cons of the proposed policy are clearly delineated, truth will emerge and the policymaker will be able to distinguish good policy from bad.

Although there is nothing morally objectionable about this argument's assumptions and conclusions, David Luban has two concerns about it. First, he argues that it is empirically dubious whether it is the truth that emerges at the end of the adversary process. Luban reminds us, for example, that after a criminal trial is over

> . . . one does not find the parties coming forth to make a clean breast of it and enlighten the world as to what *really* happened. A trial is not a quiz show with the right answer waiting in the sealed envelope.[32]

And even if partisan argument should in fact produce the truth, the mere emergence of truth is no assurance of its recognition and acceptance. Since the nonspecialist has no way of knowing which of two contradictory studies, based on theoretical models incomprehensible to the lay person, is true, he or she is as likely to support the incorrect study as the correct one. Indeed, who but an astrophysicist, for example, can decide between alternative versions of the relativistic theory of gravitation? Trusting soul that I am, I rely on the "objectivity" of the scientific community. Impartial experts, will, I assume, be able to identify the "correct" theory for me. Thus, if all astrophysicists suddenly emerged from their cocoons of objectivity as full-fledged partisans, I would experience a real crisis of confidence. To whom could I turn to ask about the relative credibility of these astrophysicists? Which one of them ought I trust to be as "scientific" (loyal to the "facts") as possible? Second, Luban fears that what the proponents of adversary expertise really want is for us to excuse zealous policy experts who go overboard in the same way that we sometimes excuse excessively zealous lawyers.

In order to show the ways in which the lawyer-policy expert analogy breaks down, Luban argues that the role of lawyer permits and even requires lawyers to perform many actions that would otherwise be morally objectionable. So long as the lawyer acts within "established constraints" upon professional behavior and does nothing illegal, he or she must "maximize the likelihood that the client will prevail."[33] Lawyers are not "morally accountable" for the ends they achieve or for the means used in the achievement of these ends.[34] Thus, a lawyer may defend the Boston Strangler or help Scrooge evict Tiny Tim's forlorn family from the only hovel they can afford. He is not morally responsible for endorsing the Boston Strangler's deeds, even if his legal skills win acquittal for the heinous murder. Nor is he morally responsible for endorsing Scrooge's cruel stinginess, even if his legal skills win Scrooge his order of eviction. What the lawyer is morally responsible for, however, is the zealous pursuit of his client's ends—using, if necessary, every legal trick of the trade to achieve those ends. The lawyer may, for example, badger hostile witnesses during cross-examination until they no longer know where Boston is, let alone who the Boston Strangler is; or he may portray Tiny Tim and his family as "loafers" and "malingerers" who deserve to be evicted.

Now, speculates Luban, if it is true that the lawyer's professional role creates an institutional excuse from certain ascriptions of moral responsibility, then perhaps similar excuses are available to all professionals. Indeed, the proponents of an adversary system of policy expertise seem to suggest that policy experts, *qua* professionals, do indeed have an institutional excuse for advocating unworthy causes. Supposedly, someone has to represent the con of every pro argument just in case the con argument is true. But aside from the fact that we do not know if verbal conflict produces truth, there is, according to David Luban, one major objection to this line of argument; namely, that an institutional excuse is only as good as its instutition. An adversary system of *criminal* justice, for example, has better credentials than an adversary system of *civil* justice. And arguably both of these systems have better credentials than an adversary system of policy advising, analyzing, and consulting.

An adversary system of criminal justice is justified because, among other things, it balances the scales between the powerless criminal-accused and the powerful state, thereby cutting down on abuses by government; because it honors basic constitutional rights; and because it exists within an elaborate procedural system to try to prevent parties from abusing the adversary process itself. An adversary system of civil justice is less justified because where one individual brings suit against another, there is no systematic asymmetry in wealth and power between the two parties that would require rules curbing the zeal of one side for the sake of the other.[35] Even less justified, if at all justified, argues Luban, is an adversarial system of policy analyzing, advising, and consulting. The expert's sole claim to legitimacy in a representative democracy is that she traffics in information that would otherwise be unavailable to elected representatives or the average citizen. She enables the democratic process to make better-informed policy decisions on technical issues than it otherwise could. Thus, if the policy expert becomes an overly zealous advocate who presents as truth exaggerated analyses or even outright disinformation, she will have no justification for her actions. Unlike the criminal justice system that aims first at the protection of the puny individual from the mighty state and then at truth, and unlike the civil justice system that seeks first to adjudicate conflicts of rights between individuals and then to promote the truth, policy expertise aims only at the truth. Thus, the legal system may tolerate half-truths in a way that the public policy network may not.

As constructed, Luban's arguments are seductive, but mainly because none of us want to bestow our blessing on policy experts who lie in order to promote their own pet projects or those of their employers. However, once we remind ourselves that the proponents of adversarial public policy mean by an advocate not an unscrupulous hired-brain but a trustworthy yet independent expert, who debates his or her own principled point of view as honestly and candidly as possible, Luban's arguments begin to lose some of their appeal. Consider in more detail, for example, the Austrian experiment in participatory democracy mentioned in Chapter 3. In 1976 the Austrian government launched an information campaign to provide both proponents and opponents of nuclear power an "equal opportunity" to present their views to the citizenry. What is most instructive for our purposes here, however, is the effect the adversary method had on the quality of the citizen discussion groups into which the Austrian population had been divided. In analyzing the role the experts played within these groups, Helga Nowotny observes that the groups whom agreed on the value of the adversary procedure fared better than the groups that did not. The discussions of the former, but not the latter, groups were characterized by "mutual respect" and in "terms of conflict management and doing justice to the substantive content of their work," their performance surpassed that of the other groups.[36] As a teacher of several courses that deal with political and moral issues, Nowotny's observations come as no surprise to me. My most memorable Philosophy of Law and Ethics classes have been populated by a representative cross section of the college's student body. Nothing is more intellectually invigorating than a sustained debate between articulate exponents of conservative, liberal, and radical viewpoints. I cannot tell you if my students learned as much as I did from these debates, but because I respected my students as principled people, every once in a while they managed to disabuse me of a foolish opinion. Unfortunately, not all of my courses have been so salutary. There have been occasions when all of my students tended to nod yes to the exact same points. Not only did we put each other to sleep, we failed to change each other's minds even once.

Another point made in rebuttal to Luban's anti-adversary stance is that it is simply not true to argue that a systematic power imbalance does not exist in the policymaking process. Joel Primack and Frank von Hippel, for example, perceive a real power iniquity between government's and industry's experts on the one hand,

and those of the people on the other hand. In particular, they believe that the executive branch of the federal government is privy to knowledge that Congress needs in order to make informed decisions on behalf of the common good.[37] In large measure, the Rathjens-Wohlstetter debate—despite its distortions—is to be preferred to expert advice behind closed executive doors. Admittedly, the Rathjens-Wohlstetter debate is not a model to emulate; but when we pause to think about the role someone like consumer-advocate Ralph Nader has played in society over the last fifteen years, we begin to appreciate the value of an independent policy expert who speaks out in opposition to government or industry experts who oftentimes have vested interests other than the common good.

Having defended an adversarial system of policy experts from Luban's blows, it occurs to me that Luban is not really against the position I have been defending for the last few paragraphs. The kind of measured debate most advocates of adversary expertise have in mind neither excuses nor justifies manipulative tricks or outright deceptions. Rather it resembles the kind of attentiveness to truth characteristic of a judge-based inquisitiorial system. Over and over again, we are reminded that the judges in the science court on in the citizens' court will solicit adequate information on both sides of the story before determining how it will end. If this is indeed the case, we can hope to avoid some of the excesses of an adversarial system that is sometimes so dedicated to process that it forgets the substantive ideals it typically espouses.

NOTES

1. Alan H. Goldman, *The Moral Foundations of Professional Ethics* (Totowa, New Jersey: Rowman and Littlefield, 1980).

2. Michael D. Bayles, *Professional Ethics* (Belmont, Calif.: Wadsworth Publishing Company, 1981), 60-70.

3. Donald F. Hornig, "The President's Need for Science Advice: Past and Future," in *Science Advice to the President*, ed. William T. Golden (New York: Pergamon Press, 1980), 43.

4. William D. Carey, "The Pleasure of Advising," in *Science Advice to the President*, ed. Golden, 97.

5. Ibid.

6. Albert Wohlstetter, "Strategy and the Natural Scientists," in *Scientists and National Policy-Making*, eds. Robert Gilpin and Christopher Wrights (New York: Columbia University Press, 1964), 191.

7. Solly Zucherman, *Nuclear Illusion and Reality* (New York: The Viking Press, 1982), 131.

8. I. I. Rabi, "The President and his Scientific Advisers," in *Science Advice to the President*, ed. Golden, 16.

9. Monroe H. Freedman, *Lawyers' Ethics in an Adversary System* (Indianapolis, Ind.: Bobbs-Merrill Co., 1975), 9.

10. Bayles, *Professional Ethics*, 70.

11. Ibid., 72.

12. Edward A. Suchman, "Action for What? A Critique of Evaluative Research," in *Evaluating Action Programs: Readings in Social Action and Education* ed. Carol Weiss (Boston: Allyn and Bacon, Inc., 1972), 81.

13. To excuse *X* is to claim that although *X* did the *wrong* action, certain circumstances undermining *X*'s knowledge and/or power mitigate *X*'s culpability. To justify *X*'s action is to claim that, despite arguments to the contrary, *X*'s action was *right*.

14. R. V. Jones, "Temptations and Risks of the Scientific Adviser," *Minerva* 10, no. 3 (July 1972), 447.

15. Ibid.

16. Ibid.

17. Bayles, *Professional Ethics*, 66–67.

18. Jones, "Temptations and Risks of the Scientific Adviser," 447.

19. Bayles, *Professional Ethics*, 76.

20. Carey, "The Pleasures of Advising," in *Science Advice to the President*, ed. Golden, 97.

21. John Burke, "The President and his Advisors: Vietnam '65," (unpublished paper, 1982), 15.

22. E. S. Quade, *Analysis for Public Decisions* (New York: American Elsevier Publishing Co., Inc., 1975), 23.

23. Operations Research Society of America, "Guidelines for the Practice of Operations Research," *Operations Research* 19, no. 5 (September 1971), 1183–84.

24. Ibid, 1185.

25. Ibid, 1170.

26. Ibid., 1171–73.

27. "The Obligations of Scientists as Counsellors," *Minera* 10, no. 1 (January 1972), 138.

28. Operations Research Society of America, "Guidelines for the Practice of Operations Research," 1218.

29. Ibid., 1134–35.

30. Paul Doty, "Can Investigations Improve Scientific Advice? The Case of the ABM," *Minerva* 10, no. 1 (January 1972), 293.

31. Ibid., 283–84.

32. David Luban, "The Adversary System Excuse," in *The Good Lawyer*, ed. David Luban (Totowa, New Jersey: Rowman & Allanheld, 1983), 93.

33. Murray Schwartz, "The Professionalism and Accountability of Lawyers," *California Law Review* 66 (1978), 673.

34. Ibid.

35. Luban, *The Good Lawyer*, 111–17.

36. Helga Nowotny, "The Role of the Experts in Developing Public Policy: The Austrian Debate on Nuclear Power," *Science, Technology, and Human Values*, 5, no. 32 (Summer 1980).

37. Joel Primack and Frank von Hippel, *Advice and Dissent: Scientists in the Political Arena* (New York: Basic Books, Inc., Publishers, 1974), 8.

Chapter 7

The Policy Expert's
Obligations to Third Parties

If policy experts bore obligations only to their policymaking clients, it would be difficult enough for them to develop the virtues of honesty, candor, competence, diligence, loyalty, and discretion. As it stands, however, policy experts also have obligations to third parties: those people who will be affected for better or for worse by the policy decisions they, the experts, help shape. Many of the most complex and controversial problems in professional ethics concern conflicts between a professional to a client and to others. For decades, professionals were trained to put the interests of their clients above everyone else's interests. Generations of lawyers, for example, were instructed that

> An advocate, in the discharge of his duty, knows but one person in all the world, and that person is his client. To save that client by all means and expedients, and at all hazards and costs to other persons, and, amongst them, to himself, is his first and only duty; and in performing this duty he must not regard the alarm, the torments, the destruction which he may bring upon others. Separating the duty of a patriot from that of an advocate, he must go on reckless of consequences, though it should be his unhappy fate to involve his country in confusion.[1]

Not to be outdone in their devotion to the client, elder physicians have instructed their younger colleagues that no matter what, the patient comes first. And so on for a variety of the most respected professions.

Tradition notwithstanding, however, the client no longer dominates the professional's consciousness. Third parties have arrived on the scene, and professionals are no longer immune from exhortations like the following: "Yes, Counselor Jones, an alleged rapist does deserve a fair trial, but not at the expense of his alleged victim. But we do not believe that you have the right to cast undeserved aspersions on the alleged victim's character in order to construct the most favorable case possible for your defendant client." And "Yes, Dr. Smith, you do have a duty to provide the woman whose fetus you are aborting with the best possible care. But what happens when the fetus is born live? Do you not bear obligations to this tiny person as well as to the one who contracted your services?"

If questions are being raised about lawyers' and physicians' obligations to third parties, however, even more questions are being raised about policy experts' obligations to persons other than their policymaking clients. As potential defendants and as potential patients, we are rather kindly disposed to the notion that lawyers and physicians have very strong professional obligations to their clients and patients respectively. But because very few of us project ourselves as policymakers, it is very difficult for us to understand how a policy expert's duty of loyalty and discretion to his or her client, for example, could possibly override the public's right to know x, y, or z. If we are prone to any extreme view, it is the view that the policy expert's obligations to third parties always trump his or her obligations to clients. However, like all other extreme views, this one is subject to scrutiny. What I propose to do in this chapter, therefore, is (1) to outline policy experts' obligations to third parties, emphasizing the virtues they should exhibit in performing these obligations; (2) to propose tests for reconciling conflicts between policy experts' obligations to their clients on the one hand and to third parties on the other hand; and (3) to outline the courses of action available to policy experts who decide that their third-party obligations are indeed heavier than their client obligations, identifying which course of action—resigning, whistle blowing, leaking—is justified under what set of circumstances.

VIRTUOUS POLICY EXPERTS: THEIR OBLIGATIONS TO THIRD PARTIES

In our discussion of the policy expert-policymaker relationship, we noted that the ground virtue of their fiduciary relationship is trustworthiness. Unless policy experts and policymakers trust each other, they will not be able to develop virtues like honesty, candor, competence, diligence, loyalty, and discretion. If I do not trust you, dare I, for example, be candid with you? The questions we must now consider are these: (1) What sort of relationship exists between policy experts and third parties, be these "third parties" specific individuals or the public at large? and (2) what virtue(s) ground this relationship?

In response to these questions, there are those who insist that the policy expert-third party relationship is nothing more or less than a person-to-person relationship. As a human person, I ought to exhibit certain virtues toward you and to fulfill certain obligations when you are concerned simply because you are another human person. These personal obligations are usually termed "ordinary obligations" by philosophers, who contrast them with special or professional obligations—additional obligations that a person assumes by entering into contractual or quasi-contractual relationships with other persons. Given this way of dividing up the world of obligations, policy experts have an ordinary obligation of justice, for example, to us as well as to their policymaking clients. They are no more justified in cheating us than in cheating their clients. Policy experts are justified, however, in being less candid with us than with their clients. Human persons are not ordinarily obligated to fully disclose all information to each other in all their dealings. Were such an obligation incumbent on one and all, all the fun would be taken out of bargaining for merchandise at a bazaar. However, once a person decides to become a policy expert, he or she is bound to disclose all relevant information to his or her policymaking client. Candor is one of the rules that governs the game of policy analyzing and advising.

If it is true to claim, as was claimed above, that policy experts have a person-to-person relationship with third parties, then what virtue(s) ground this basic relationship? Depending on which philosopher we consult, a slightly different list of virtues will emerge. Fortunately, despite their quibblings over the fine points, most philosophers agree that absent the virtues of justice and benevolence, people could not and would not live together. Imagine a world in which people lied to each other at random, failed to treat similar cases similarly, harmed each other at whim, and gave nary a thought to each other's pleasure and pains. It is difficult to call such a world a society. Being a professional, therefore, in no way exempts a person from his or her ordinary obligations; rather, it simply adds to his or her moral burdens.

Although I do not deny that the policy expert-third party relationship is a person-to-person relationship, I do believe that it is somewhat misleading to speak as if it is *only* a person-to-person relationship. What I am suggesting is that the policy expert-third party relationship has some quasi-professional dimensions. By no means is this an entirely original point. It has been made in the past and forcefully so. For example, in a 1970 protest about the volume of various contracts for research and analysis let to the New York City Rand Institute, the New York City Council raised the following issues:

> When a consultant works for government, who is the client? Is it the executive branch which engages him, or the legislative body which raises the funds to pay him, or the citizen whose stake in his work may be far more vital than a stockholder's interest in a private corporation?
>
> The consultants presently employed by the city and the agencies which retain them believe beyond any question that the client is the executive branch of government.
>
> We conclude, however, that the client is not solely the executive branch, but the legislature as well and ultimately the city's citizens. It cannot be otherwise in a free society.[2]

The New York City Council's conclusions make particular sense if we reassess the policy expert's professional obligations to his or her policymaking client. Are these obligations owed (1) to the *person* of the client, (2) to the office or department the policymaker heads, or (3) to the people who directly elected or indirectly appointed him or her? In other words, are the policy expert's professional obligations directed

(1) to *Mr. Jones*, who happens to be Secretary of State, (2) to the *office of the Secretary of State*, which Mr. Jones happens to occupy, or (3) to the people who voted in the administration that appointed Mr. Jones?

The answer to this question is a surprising "all of the above." The reason why policy experts have professional obligations to policymakers is because without them, policymakers would have a difficult time forging enlightened public policy on our behalf. Because it is in our best interest, we approve of a system whereby experts burden themselves with special obligations to policymakers, even though we realize that by so doing we will have to say "All well and good" on those occasions when the policy expert's threefold professional duties supercede his or her ordinary duties to us. In the same way that we do not always require doctors or lawyers to rank their professional obligation of confidentiality to their clients lower than their ordinary obligation to truth telling to us, we do not always require policy experts to put their ordinary obligations above their professional obligations.

Significantly, however, the analogy between doctors and lawyers on the one hand and policy experts on the other hand is far from perfect. Whereas the patient in the hospital or the defendant in the courtroom is the immediate and ultimate client of the doctor and lawyer respectively, the policymaker is merely the *immediate* recipient of the policy expert's services. He or she is the proxy of the people who are the *ultimate* recipients of the policy expert's services. If this were a much simpler, smaller, and direct democracy, in which all competent adults voted on every single public policy issue, then the policy experts would bring their information directly to the people. As it stands, however, this is a very complex, large, and representative democracy in which policy experts communicate with policymakers on the assumption that these policymakers are literally the people's substitutes.

Thus, what is most wrong with the agency model of the policy expert-policymaker relationship, for example, is that it suggests that this relationship is analogous not so much to that between trial lawyers and their defendant clients as to that between "expert witnesses for hire" and their defendant clients. According to many critics, the hired-expert system is the most scandalous part of our legal system. David Luban, for example, cites with particular disapproval the "trained-seal psychiatrists" at the Hinckley trial and the notorious Texas "Doctor Death" who finds every murderer psychiatrically suitable for capital punishment.[3]

Bad though it is to compare the policy expert-policymaker relationship with that between expert witnesses for hire and defendant-clients, it is even worse, though possibly more germane, to compare this professional relationship with the one between expert witnesses for hire and *corporate* defendant-clients. Paid economic experts in antitrust cases can earn up to $4000 a day in consulting fees to demonstrate that the effects of a corporation's activities on competition are whatever the client claims them to be:

> In theory, the testimony of such an expert is supposed to represent the independent judgment of the expert, untainted by favoritism toward either party. In practice, the economists, who otherwise subsist on academic salaries, know

to whom they owe their six-figure yearly incomes. Highly respected experts have been known to ask lawyers, "Tell me what I'm supposed to say."[4]

Although policy experts who labor in the public sector work not for corporations (individuals supposedly bent on maximizing their profits) but for the government (individuals supposedly bent on serving the best interests of the people), they are subject to the same temptations that their private-sector peers are. For a price, some public policy experts can forget the fact that their professional obligations are not to the policymaker's personal interests—for example, increased power or reelection—but to the people's best interests, the interests the policymaker is committed to serve. When they join the government bureaucracy, policy experts commit themselves to the state as an abstract repository of all the values of society. Like the policymakers who hire them, they must "put loyalty to the highest moral principles and to the country above loyalty to persons, party, or Government department."[5] Thus, when we speak of a conflict between a policy expert's "professional obligations" to his or her policymaking client on the one hand and his or her ordinary obligations to third parties on the other hand, as in the case of some "hired brains," we may really be speaking of a more fundamental moral tug-of-war—the one between duty to others, be they clients or third parties, and raw self-interest.

ON RECONCILING IMAGINED OR REAL CONFLICTS OF OBLIGATIONS: THE TRIALS AND TRIBULATIONS OF THE VIRTUOUS POLICY EXPERT

Obligation Versus Self-Interest

As we just noted above, sometimes what is described as a conflict between a policy expert's professional obligations to third parties is better understood as a conflict between self-interest and duty. Sometimes policy experts are only too willing to ignore obligations, professional and/or ordinary, in order to promote their own self-interest directly and/or indirectly. A case in point is the 1958-69 cyclamates controversy reported by Joel Primack and Frank von Hippel.[6]

Policy experts—in this case chemists, biologists, and especially medical doctors—played a key role in several maneuvers which (1) led the Food and Drug Administration (FDA) to classify cyclamates as "Generally Recognized as Safe" (GRAS) for over ten years; (2) prompted Robert Finch, Secretary of Health, Education, and Welfare (HEW) to conclude in 1969 that the benefits of cyclamates outweighed the risks; and (3) led a new Secretary of HEW, scarcely a year later, to reverse Finch's decision, banning cyclamates entirely.

Despite the fact that many FDA experts strongly suspected that several adverse effects were associated with the frequent ingestion of cyclamates (e.g., growth retardation, liver damage, chromosomal damage, and birth defects), the FDA was reluctant to mount a federal case on these suspicions. Very few, if any, FDA officials wanted to fight either the manufacturers of very lucrative diet drinks and food or the millions of plump Americans who believed, rightly or wrongly, that cyclamates would swiftly and sweetly deliver them from the tyranny of fat. Unfortunately—for the FDA, that is—the food industry is constituted not only by those who sell "slimming" cyclamates but also by those who market "fattening" sugar. As a result of a laboratory study conducted by the Sugar Research Foundation, it was discovered that cyclamates produce bladder cancer in rats. This finding activated the Delaney Clause, a section of the Food Additives Amendment which mandates that if a food additive is shown to produce cancer in man or animal, it is to be deemed unsafe. Once the Delaney Clause was activated, the FDA was legally bound to ban cyclamates; it had no other choice.[7]

Not to be defeated, however, then Secretary of HEW Finch thought he could create another option for the FDA, whose offices reside within HEW. Were cyclamates redescribed as "nonprescription drugs" and moved to appropriate supermarket shelves, they could escape the noose of the Delaney Clause. Scarcely had Finch finished congratulating himself, however, than the FDA came to its senses, pointing out that this ploy would not work since cyclamates could not be registered as a drug unless their manufacturers could prove them both to be safe and effective against some disease. But, given the bladder cancer studies and evidence suggesting that cyclamates, far from waging a successful battle against the "disease" of obesity, may actually contribute to it by stimulating ingesters' appetites, the cyclamates industry was hard pressed to come up with the needed proof for safety and effectiveness.[8]

Somewhat of an eternal optimist, Finch did not let the FDA have the final word. He promptly set up the secretary's Medical Advisory Committee on Cyclamates. Whether it was the secretary's blessing they wanted or the lucrative and prestigious government jobs he could provide, this handpicked group of policy experts, many of them medical doctors, found Finch all the evidence he needed to rehabilitate cyclamates as nonprescription drugs. Pooh-poohing both the new bladder cancer reports and the old evidence that birth defects and genetic damage were related to cyclamates, the committee claimed that cyclamates were particularly effective in managing juvenile diabetes, "where sweets and soft drinks are a special problem."[9]

Finch's ploy notwithstanding, Ralph Nader blew the whistle on cyclamates in a report entitled *The Chemical Feast*. Largely as a result of his probings, the FDA stood firm, refusing to rubber-stamp the findings of Finch's advisory committee. Shortly thereafter Finch left, or was asked to leave, HEW. A politically astute person, his successor realized that he had to ban cyclamates or else. To this end, he assembled the *very same* Medical Advisory Committee on Cyclamates, apparently insisting that they reverse their previous findings. No dummies, the policy experts did just this. Citing "new information"—which was in fact the same old information that had been around for some time—the committee found that, after all, cyclamates were neither safe nor effective. In their analysis of the cyclamates decision, Primack and von Hippel sum it up all too well when they observe that "the prostitution of the advisory committee system in this case is obvious and needs no further comment."[10]

Like Primack and von Hippel, I have no desire to belabor the obvious. Nevertheless, I do wish to underscore one point about this case. Had the policy experts on the Medical Advisory Committee not been looking out for their own self-interest, they may have failed less miserably as moral agents. As it so happened, they chose self-interest over any and all of their obligations. Failing to exercise their bona fide professional obligations to Finch by being less than honest and candid with him and by working in less than a competent or diligent manner on the cyclamates question, they decided to exercise what amounted to pseudo obligations of loyalty and discretion.

Significantly, even if the members of the Medical Advisory Committee had tried to fulfill all their bona fide professional obligations, they would still have had to weigh them against such ordinary obligations as justice and benevolence. What the record shows, however, is that the experts paid little, if any, attention to their ordinary obligations. They violated truthfulness by withholding the facts about cyclamates from the American public; they violated nonmaleficence by putting the American public at risk of cancer; and they violated fairness by giving the cyclamates industry an edge over the sugar industry. Clearly, the advisory committee was bent on maximizing its interests rather than those of the people. So far was duty from the experts' mind that their actions can be neither excused nor justified.

Professional Obligations Versus Ordinary Obligations

Cases like the cyclamates controversy are not nearly as interesting as cases in which policy experts do struggle to weigh their bona fide professional obligations against some of their pressing ordinary obligations. Such excruciating exercises in ethics occur both when the third parties in question are particular individuals and when they constitute the public at large.

The Moral Perils of Social Experimentation. Sometimes the policy expert's professional obligations of competence and diligence, for example, conflict with his or her ordinary obligations of truthfulness, nonmaleficence, and fairness. This frequently happens in the context of so-called social experimentation, which seeks to measure the effects of changes in policy variables by applying these changes to human populations under conditions of controlled experimentation similar to those used in the physical and biological sciences. Whereas controlled experiments in the physical and biological sciences are usually designed to test the effects of particular natural substances, however, social experiments are designed to measure the likely effects of projected social programs.

Although social experimentation is riddled with a host of problems—for example, the time element (anywhere from one to two years of preparation, two to ten years of field experimentation, and one to three years of analysis), the space element (regional biases), and the cost element (millions)—it may well be justified:

> If a fundamental policy change is under consideration, and if there is no clear basis for estimating a priori the effect of this policy on economic behavior, then the only way to obtain this information is to put the policy into practice on a limited scale and see what happens. This is especially so if there is reason

to believe the policy change could have strong negative as well as positive effects.[11]

Whether social experimentation is justified from a moral point of view as well as from a political and economic perspective, however, is another matter. In this connection, let us consider the Denver Income Maintenance Experiment (DIME), ably summarized by Dennis F. Thompson in *Ethics and Politics*.[12] DIME was the last in a series of four government-sponsored studies designed to discover to what extent, if any, recipients of a guaranteed income would change their behavior. Would they, for example, work less? Would guaranteed incomes destroy the Protestant work ethic once and for all?

In order to answer these questions appropriately, the Colorado Department of Social Services, which had been contracted by HEW, subcontracted the Stanford Research Institute (SRI) and Mathematica Policy Research (MPR). During the preliminary planning stages, SRI proposed a 20-year study instead of the usual three- or five-year study. Its proposal was based on the reasonable assumption that most people will not change their behavior dramatically if they know that the right hand of government will soon take away what the left hand has given. I, for one, would not quit my job if I knew, or strongly suspected, that the government would, after a few years or so, stop sending the gravy train around. Who is irrational enough to live as if the next three years of life are the only years of life left? Such behavior may make sense if one expects to die or to commit suicide within a three-year period; otherwise, it's foolhardy at best and positively crazy at worse. On the other hand, if the government promises to take care of me and mine for the next 20 years, then if I am between the ages of 35 and 55, I am very likely to take full advantage of its offer. Why, I may even give that job up after all!

The 20-year plan caught on at HEW. At first there was some question as to whether the experiment really had to run its full 20-year course. Wasn't it enough simply to convince the subject participants that the program would last 20 years when, in point of fact, it would be terminated at the end of five years with some sort of severance pay? After much discussion at HEW, it was decided that this was not an ethically acceptable way to proceed, especially because people who enrolled in a 20-year plan might

1. Take on long-range debt commitments;
2. Decide to have more children than they otherwise would;
3. Decide on early retirement; or
4. Decide to forgo savings or life insurance.[13]

Thus, the undersecretary of HEW gave an order in 1974 to commence a bona fide 20-year study.

Initially, 110 families were enrolled in DIME. But this sample rapidly grew to 195 families for two reasons: (1) Not enough families in the original sample earned little enough to benefit from the DIME payments, and (2) no Mexican-Americans, who constitute a sizable percentage of Denver's population, had been enrolled in the program. Although all the families who ultimately enrolled in DIME signed an agreement which stipulated that the government intended to continue the program for 20 years "subject to modification,"[14] the MPR staff, who were in charge of the sign-up, were told that it was of "crucial importance to the success of the experiment"[15] that the subject participants *believe* in the 20-year guarantee. Four years into the experiment it became clear that, for a variety of reasons we need not discuss here, the 20-year study was of "no research value."[16] Policymakers at HEW were convinced that the program should be terminated. Policy experts at SRI concurred with HEW, arguing, however, that although no one involved was *legally* obligated to make good on DIME's promises, everyone involved was *morally* obligated to assure the families that they would be "no worse off as a result of DIME participation than if they had not participated at all."[17] The policy experts at MPR echoed the sentiments of their SRI colleagues, insisting that the government provide each participant family with a lump sum payment equaling what HEW would have paid them over the remaining 15 years. HEW policymakers, however, thought that this was not only a poor option but a costly one at that: $9.17 million. They outlined at least two other options—termination with lump sum payments less than $9.17 million and termination with transition payments less than $9.17 million. Ultimately HEW decided on a three-year declining payment option totalling $1.47 million.

This case is instructive in several respects. What I would like to focus on here, however, are the ethical problems surrounding the *initiation* rather than the *termination* of DIME. The first problem surrounds the virtue of truthfulness. Grave ethical concerns have been expressed about social experiments that center around the related issues of informed consent and deception. People have a right to know what is likely to happen to them when and if they sign on the dotted line. Only in this way can they have some control over their own destiny. Unfortunately, policy experts, intent on performing competently and diligently, are well aware that the less information they provide and the lower level of consent they demand, the better chance they have of securing ideal subjects for their studies. Deception, then, takes on the cast of the noble lie: Unless we lie to the people on this occasion, we cannot benefit them on other occasions. For example, although there is no proof of any wrongdoing on the part of the SRI or MPR policy experts—in fact, to the contrary—they may have been tempted to convey with too much fervor the impression that only a nuclear war would interfere with the 20-year payment schedule of DIME. To the end of securing a necessary goal—that is, believing participants—they may have supplied potential participants with misleading information, withheld information, or both. In the course of conducting medical experiments, physicians face an analogous problem when, for example, they provide a control group with a placebo and an experimental group with the real drug. If the physicians tell the experimental subjects that 50 percent of them will receive the real drug and 50 percent of them will receive the placebo, the experiment will not work as well as one in which everyone is convinced that he or she is receiving the real drug. But, we may ask, is it right to fool people, even if the information secured by fooling them ultimately benefits them?

Policy experts, who are less than truthful with social experiment participants, often justify their decision to lie deliberately or to withhold information on utilitarian grounds. They reason as follows: "Admittedly, a women who thinks that she will be receiving generous government subsidies for twenty years may decide to have more children than she otherwise would. This decision puts her at risk of harm because if the government kills the 'golden goose,' she may find herself in the position of Old Mother Hubbard with nothing in her cupboard. Still, while the government is filling her cupboard, she is being benefited in ways that she would not have been benefited otherwise. Moreover, society as a whole, and in particular the social class she represents, benefits from her participation in the social experiment. Without participating subjects like her, society could not gain important knowledge. Therefore, if the only way to get this woman to participate as an ideal subject is to assure her that golden eggs will indeed be delivered for the next twenty years, then the deception may indeed be justified. Anyway, for all we know, the woman may not decide to have more children than she otherwise would!"

According to the followers of Kant, whom we met in Chapter 5, the problem with any such utilitarian line of reasoning is that it can easily turn into a glib rationalization for treating a person like the proverbial guinea pig. Thus, policy experts have to ask themselves whether alternatives to social experimentation exist—alternatives that do not involve lying, harm doing, or injustice. Sissela Bok notes that there are at least three alternatives to ethically dubious social experiments: (1) Forgo the knowledge sought; (2) seek the knowledge nonexperimentally, by studying records and other forms of data; and (3) pursue the knowledge experimentally, but by laying all the cards out on the table.[18] Admittedly, there will be cases where all these alternatives fail. If so, the policy expert should not automatically assume that it is absolutely wrong to go ahead with his or her original plan, for as Robert Rosenthal has observed:

> The behavioral researcher whose study might reduce violence or racism or sexism, but who refuses to do the study because it involves deception, has not solved an ethical problem but only traded it in for another.[19]

Perhaps there is no single rule, then, that covers permissible versus impermissible uses of social experimentation. On occasion, the policy expert will have to make a judgment call. Still in all, *prima facie* assumption should be against proceeding, even in the absence of alternatives, if subject participants are going to be deceived and perhaps even harmed. Margaret Mead spoke with considerable wisdom when she reminded us that

> ... Encouraging styles of research and intervention that involve lying to other human beings. . . tends to establish a corps of progressively calloused individuals, insulated from self-criticism and increasingly available for clients who can become outspokenly cynical in their manipulating of other human beings, individually and in the mass.[20]

In sum, policy experts have to remember that in choosing for themselves, they choose for others. On the one hand, if they get carried away with doing their job to the best of their ability, with producing statistically significant results at almost any cost, then policy experts will project an image of themselves as heartless brains. On the other hand, if policy experts become paralyzed, for example, at the mere thought of telling even the whitest of lies to one of their subject participants, then they will project an image of themselves as ineffectual and indecisive do-gooders.

Policy experts, who realize that any image of themselves either as number-crunching drones or as tortured intellectuals are ethically undesirable—the first because it leads to an attitude of "I am the controller, you are the controllee," the second because it leads to an attitude of "I am just a drop in an ocean of helpless hopelessness"—may benefit from Bruce Jennings's and Robert Bellah's work in the area of so-called interpretive social science.

We discussed Jennings's distinctions between "positivistic" and "interpretive" social science in Chapter 2. His distinctions are strengthened by Bellah's contrast between "technical" and "practical" social science. As Bellah sees it, a technical social science is "proud." It promises a genuine science of human behavior on the model of modern natural sciences, true in all possible worlds, and in order to make good on its promise it produces instruments toward the *understanding* of society. In contrast, a practical social science is "humble." It does not promise the scientific precision to which technical social science aspires, and it produces instruments toward the *self-understanding* of society. Practical social scientists do not set themselves up against the "objects" they study, claim to be able to predict exactly the outcomes of alternative policies, or present their findings in the form of lawlike generalizations. They know better. Comments Bellah:

> If the limitations of technological social science were clearly understood neither politicians and administrators on the one hand nor "troubled persons" and "human resources" professionals on the other could claim the legitimating authority of science for their opinions or decisions. Technical knowledge would be viewed as only one rather uncertain input into a situation that also requires common sense, ethical insight, and a great deal of conversation with those affected before a policy can be formulated or a decision made. The important point is that technical knowledge does not necessitate anything. Decisions and commitments must emerge from the practical context of communicative action.[21]

Although some policy experts—especially those with backgrounds in the social sciences—are concerned that policymakers will have no use for them once everyone realizes that science has its limits, this is no reason for policy experts to pretend that the situation is otherwise. Rather, it is probably time for policy experts to admit that technical reasoning is only one sort of reasoning, and a limited one at that. To the degree that technical reasoning is suited to the natural sciences, which study natural phenomena in order to control them, it is not suited to the social sciences, which study human persons in order to liberate them. This is why Jennings's distinction between positivistic and interpretive social science and Bellah's distinction between technical and practical social science are so important. It makes a difference whether policy experts conceive of persons as objects or subjects. Comments Jennings:

> There is a symbiotic relationship between a mode of social scientific explanation which defines human agents as objects whose behavior is determined by causal forces and a form of government which relies on the instrumental manipulation of those forces for the achievement of social objectives and the maintenance of social order.[22]

If Jennings is right, then there may also be a symbiotic relationship between a mode of social scientific explanation that defines human beings as self-directing and self-controlling agents and a form of government that relies on the informed participation of those agents for the achievement of mutually agreed-upon social objectives and the maintenance not merely of social order but of human community.

Thus, if policy experts are really interested in using their expertise for the common good, then they will think a hundred times before engaging in a mode of social experimentation that is in any way, shape, or form manipulative. The policy expert who makes it a habit to think in "interpretive" and "practical" terms rather than in "positivistic" and "technical" terms will make less mistakes in balancing his or her professional obligations of competence and diligence against his or her ordinary obligations of truthfulness, nonmaleficence, and fairness. Virtue is as much a state of mind as a mode of decision making and action performing.

The Moral Perils of Invoking the Common Good. Perhaps the most serious conflicts between professional and ordinary obligations occur when the obligations of loyalty and discretion (understood as confidentiality) to policymaking clients fail to mesh with the obligations of truthfulness and nonmaleficence to third parties. Many professionals treasure the principle of confidentiality. Lawyers, psychiatrists, and doctors, for example, promise those who seek their services that their communications will be kept in confidence. This promised confidentiality, however, is not absolute and there are restrictions on what it properly covers. Lawyers are currently permitted, though not required, to reveal a client's intention to murder someone; psychiatrists are required to reveal a serious danger of violence threatened by their patients; and doctors are generally permitted, and even required, to reveal teenaged pregnancies. What dictates the strength and "appropriate scope" of a profession's obligations of confidentiality will depend on the answers to the following three questions: (1) How important to society is the profession's purpose? (2) to achieve this purpose, what degree of candor is necessary between the client and the professional? and (3) how strict must the ties of loyalty and discretion, understood as confidentiality, be before the client and the professional trust each other enough to speak their minds freely?[23]

When we have in mind professions like medicine and law, it is relatively easy to answer such questions. The goals of health for all and of justice for all are very important to society; and, without candor, doctors, psychiatrists and lawyers would not be able to serve their respective clients well. Will I bare my soul to a psychiatrist if I suspect that he or she will trumpet-blast my hidden weaknesses to his or her cocktail-party guests? Will I reveal embarrassing facts about my body to someone who will disclose them at whim or overreadily to my employer? Will I tell my lawyer the whole truth and nothing but the truth if I know that he or she will tattle on me to the authorities? Of course not. Thus I need to know that my psychiatrist, doctor, and lawyer will exhibit the virtues of loyalty and discretion when it comes to me and my affairs. However, when it comes to a profession like policy analysis, does its goals of informed public policy depend in any major way on the candor that exists between policy experts and their policymaking clients; and, in turn, to what degree is this candor dependent on a trust relationship between those in the know and those in power?

In addressing this last question, it is important to note that in a recent anthology, *Science Advice to the President*, policy experts as well as their policymaking clients repeatedly claimed that, absent mutual trust, they could not do business with each other. What is most striking about this anthology is the number of times words like "loyalty" and "discretion" appear; and the three major arguments that are constructed in favor of strict confidentiality between policy experts and policymakers—a confidentiality akin to that which rules doctor-patient and lawyer-client conversations.

The first of these arguments claims that policy experts must be protected from retaliation or pressure. Because their advice is so valuable, policy experts should be spared every possible indignity, insult, and injury. They should not be persecuted like Oppenheimer was because of his unpopular advice on strategic weapons, supposedly given in private; and they should not be harassed like those Columbia University professors who received threatening telephone calls and hate mail because of their work on weapons technology for the Vietnam War. The second argument insists that policymakers must be able to have frank and open discussions with experts during the policymaking process. Supposedly, if policymaking deliberations are open to the press and public, neither the policy experts nor the policymakers will feel free to say what they really think for fear that it will be misunderstood, misapplied, or used against them. Subjected to such constraints, the quality of discourse will erode and the resultant policies will be anemic versions of what they might have been. Finally, the third argument claims that we must assure confidentiality of advice and information relating to military and industrial technology, since it could be of use to a potential enemy or simple competitor. Material must be classified in order to preserve national security.[24]

Weighty as these arguments may be, they are rebuttable. In the first place, although neither the persecution nor the harassment of unpopular policy experts is justifiable or even excusable, policy experts should be held accountable for the advice they give. If they are unwilling to take public responsibility for their participation in government decision making, and if they are unwilling to share with outsiders the information they are willing to communicate to insiders, there is no check—not even that of professional societies, let alone that of the press or of the people—on what plans they suggest or fail to suggest. Second, even though some confusion would inevitably accompany the public's full access to every policy discussion, it is not clear that this admittedly harmful consequence of more widely shared knowledge is any more harmful to us than living in a society where a Star Chamber's proceedings are insulated from our scrutiny. Third, and finally, although material must at times be kept secret in the interest of the national defense or foreign policy, the present system of "security classification" is a bureaucratic nightmare. So much material has been overclassified that even the Defense Department's own Science Board Task Force has admitted that "the volume of scientific and technical information that is classified could profitably be decreased by perhaps as much as 90 percent through limiting the amount of information classified and the deviation of its classification."[25] Seeming reforms like former President Nixon's executive order mandating "automatic" declassification of documents promise more than they deliver. Documents that are classified "confidential" (the lowest security classification) must wait six years before they are "automatically" declassified; and even this simple declassification is subject to bureaucratic review, the final authority in case of disputes over classification being the Interagency Classification Review Committee, consisting of members of the agencies that originally classified the documents.

When we reflect on the struggle between those who favor strict rules of confidentiality between policy experts and policymakers and those who favor few, if any, such rules, we begin to understand why it is misleading to compare the relationship between doctors and patients or the relationship between lawyers and defendant-clients with that between policy experts and policymakers. Patients and defendant-clients are extremely vulnerable people. They are individuals operating from a position of weakness who hope that their doctors can cure them of their physical and mental infirmities or who hope that their lawyers can keep them out of prison. In contrast, policymakers generally operate from a position of strength. The policymaker who uses a policy expert is not to be compared to a failing student who hires a tutor but to a graduate student who consults with the experts in the field. Likewise, the policymaker who confides in his or her staff is not to be compared to a penitent who confesses to a priest. Policymakers are not in the habit of sharing personal intimacies with their policy experts. On those occasions when a policymaker does share a secret with a policy expert, that policy expert owes the same ordinary obligation of confidentiality to him or her as to any one of us, for as Sissela Bok has argued,

> Without a premise supporting a measure of individual control over [the degree of secrecy and openness about] personal matters, it would be impossible to preserve the indispensable respect for identity, plans, action, and belongings that all of us need and should legitimately be able to claim.[26]

The only kind of information that the policy expert usually has a professional obligation to keep confidential is that which could jeopardize national security if known by the wrong people under conditions of civil war, foreign invasion, imminent attack, terrorist threat, or other emergency. If the policy expert has any duty to third parties, it is that of nonmaleficence. Thus, before breaking confidence, policy experts must weigh the harm of the public's knowing too much too soon against the harm of its knowing too little too late.

SILENCE, DISSENTING, RESIGNING,
WHISTLE BLOWING, LEAKING:
SOME HARD CHOICES

Policy experts who are always able to harmonize their obligations to policymaking clients with their obligations to third parties are rare. There is enormous pressure to be a yes-man, to go along with the policymaking client. Although some critics believe that the best way to meet this pressure is head-on, with a loud "power to the people," it is not clear that a no-man is what policymakers need. The policymaker is no more likely to listen to an obstructionist policy expert than to ignore a syncophantic one. Thus, from the public's point of view, the best policy expert is a "yes, . . . but" man—someone who has the policymaker's trust, but someone who is, first and foremost, the servant of the people. "Yes, it's good to build up the aeronautics industry, but a fleet of SSTs will increase the earth's cloud cover or deplete its protective layer of stratospheric ozone"; "Yes, it's good if our boys are able to see North Vietnamese troop movements in South Vietnam, but the defoliant 2,4,5-T will cause many birth defects"; "Yes, it's good to have more military power than the Soviets, but a nuclear war is not winnable."

Admittedly, "yes . . . but" men sometimes have to choose between their "yesses" and their "buts." Under a certain set of circumstances, a "but" can easily mutate into a "no." The policy expert who knows, for example, that promised nuclear waste cleanups are just that—promises—may ultimately have to choose between saying "yes" and saying "no," between "putting up and shutting up" on the one hand and "going public" by means of resigning, whistle blowing, or leaking on the other.

Such choices are difficult to make, particularly when one's career is at stake, when one has been trained to be a technician and not a politician, and when one is not absolutely certain either about one's facts or about one's values. When experts, for example, spoke out against SSTs, they were not sure to what extent a fleet of SSTs would increase the earth's cloud cover or deplete its protective layer of stratospheric ozone; and when they spoke out against 2,4,5-T, they could not say precisely how many birth defects would occur in South Vietnam from its massive use there as a defoliant. In the face of such reasonable doubt, an expert might well ask himself or herself: "Is this a false alarm? Am I overstepping my role? Am I unnecessarily agitating my fellow citizens? Am I misperceiving the policymaker's motivations? Do I really see the total picture?"[27]

Under such conditions, the answer to these questions hinges on the answer to a more basic question: In situations of uncertainty, who should determine whether the benefits and opportunities of a proposed policy exceed the risks and costs? The policymakers alone? The policy expert? The people? Reporting on the safety of underground nuclear weapons testing, one PSAC panel, whose report was subsequently suppressed, suggested that:

> . . . the public should not be asked to accept risks resulting from purely internal governmental decisions if, without endangering national security, the information can be made public and the decisions reached after public discussion.[28]

Thus, even if the dangers that concern a policy expert might not materialize, the public should have an opportunity to express its opinion as to whether the potential risks and costs are worth the benefits and opportunities.

This does not mean that every matter should be made the subject of a national referendum. Normally, elected policymakers, as representatives of the people's interests, assign relative weights to the costs, benefits, risks, and opportunities of various policy alternatives. The people are simply too busy to express their opinion on every policy decision. But when policymakers know neither what the people want nor what they need and when their policy experts are in disagreement with each other or them, then policymakers should, if the matter is serious enough, consult the people. If policymakers fail to turn to the people in such situations, then their policy experts should. Without adequate information, the people cannot govern themselves.

Of course, if structures existed that permitted ordinary citizens to share directly the policy expert's knowledge and the policymaker's power, they would become coresponsible with them for the contours of public policy. Although critics of coresponsibility fear that it is a quixotic if not idiotic notion, proponents of it insist that either a pluralist model or a participatory model could safely guide the creation of effective, yet open, policy-advising structures.[29]

The pluralistic model comes close to what has been tried, though rather half-heartedly, in this country. As a result of the Freedom of Information Act and the Federal Advisory Committee Act of 1972, self-selected groups of citizens were to be given an opportunity to criticize, challenge, and contribute to public policy. Unfortunately, things did not work out as well as had been expected, and this for two reasons.

In the first place, these acts proved to be toothless tigers or fangless cobras. Of the nine exemption clauses attached to the Freedom of Information Act, for example, only one of them, exemption 1, which may withhold from the public "national defense or foreign policy matters regarded as secret and so classified," is clearly constitutional.[30] The other eight exemptions, however, do not seem to derive either from constitutional national-security considerations that give rise to secrecy and censorship, or from constitutional privacy considerations that give rise to slander and libel laws. Nevertheless, they unnecessarily keep information from the public. For example, exemptions 4, 8, and 9, which arise out of a legitimate concern to protect private property interests—"trade secrets," "information on the operation and regulation of financial institutions," and so forth—have been invoked by the Food and Drug Administration to close meetings in which the safety and effectiveness of particular drugs are discussed on the grounds that among the relevant information are "trade secrets." And for similar reasons the Atomic Energy Commission has at least partially closed meetings in which the safety and effectiveness of particular nuclear reactors are discussed.[31]

But even if acts such as the Freedom of Information Act were strengthened, this would not solve the two basic problems that trouble the pluralist model: elitism and lack of accountability. First, most special interest groups are composed not of ordinary citizens but of highly educated and politically sophisticated persons who represent various (predominently economic) sectors of society. Regrettably, not all of these special interest groups are as altruistic as Nader's raiders. Indeed, some of them are hopelessly self-interested. Second, the presence of even a limited number of self-selected special interest groups may erode accountability. Faced with a gaggle of contending groups, policymakers and/or policy experts may be tempted to play them off against one another, blaming all of them for whatever policies are adopted or—what is more likely—for the stalemates that produce no policy at all.

In contrast to the pluralist model, the participatory model largely overcomes the problem of elitism. This model, which requires policymakers to recruit ordinary citizens to participate in policymaking, takes its inspiration from the Equal Opportunity Act of 1964, which called for "maximum feasible participation" of the poor in the planning and conduct of programs designed to reduce poverty.[32] Unfortunately, to the degree that this model de-escalates the problem of elitism, it escalates the problem of accountability. Not only is it difficult for society to ascribe responsibility where the agents' number is legion, it is also difficult for inexperienced citizens to resist the blandishments of policymakers and policy experts who could, if they wished, easily co-opt them. Still, the problem of unwieldy numbers could be assuaged by decentralizing the policymaking process, and the problem of co-optation could be minimized by educating citizens prior to their participation on a given board or council. Indeed, as we noted in Chapter 4, some participatory experiments in Sweden, Austria, and the Netherlands suggest that even in science policy, citizen advisory councils can be effective if their members have the benefit of educational programs; I see no reason why the government could not require, as an alternative form of military service, say, preparation for and participation on a public policy advisory council.

But even if an open system of structures is put in place, all the policy expert's moral dilemmas will not evaporate. On occasion, he will be put into situations that open structures are not meant to handle—for example, exemption 1 situations which involve "national defense or foreign policy matters regarded as secrets and so classified."[33] What should policy experts do if they have good reason to believe that policy x will either in the long run or the short run inflict major or minor harm on the public? Under such circumstances, should policy experts remain quiet, dissent internally, resign with or without additional protest, whistle-blow without resigning, or leak without resigning?

We have already rejected absolute silence as an unacceptable course of conduct characteristic of the sycophant. In Chapter 4, however, we noted that internal dissent is easier in theory than it is in practice. Here we should recall Chester Cooper's Walter Mitty fantasies, which had a way of evaporating in the presence of Lyndon Baines Johnson. It is one thing for David to dream of taking on Goliath and quite another for him to release his slingshot. Nevertheless, most ethicists agree that when policy experts are convinced that the majority's utilities are being ignored and/or that a minority's rights are being violated, it is best that they begin by expressing their dissent internally, in the hope that the policymakers for whom they work will change their own minds about possibly or probably harmful policy *x*. It is morally preferable to give wrongdoers a chance to mend their ways because they *want to* and not simply because they *have to* for fear of negative repercussions like public censor or imprisonment.

In support of those who favor internal dissent as the first and hopefully the last court of appeals is a recent survey conducted in the private sector by David Ewing. Ewing found that over 60 percent of the business firms responding to his questionnaire claimed that they had some type of "open door" policy.[34] Supposedly, business managers—especially senior executives—have found that it is often in their own best interests and that of their corporation to encourage internal criticism. If what is good for the goose is really good for the gander, then what works in the private sector may also work in the public sector. Like business managers, policymakers may have much to gain by fostering not only "yes . . . but" men, but genuine naysayers.

According to Sissela Bok, "open door" policies succeed when they are taken seriously, when their results are publicized, and when dissenters are rewarded. These same policies fail when they are mere window dressing, when their results are kept a secret between the policymaker and the policy expert, and when dissenters are punished in countless ways—generally by assigning them trivial jobs or wearing down their confidence.[35] These policies also fail—and cruelly so—when policymakers use their "open door" policy as a Venus flytrap. "Come into my office," beckons Mr. Spider. "Tell me all your concerns. Oh, you don't say? Well, we won't be needing the services of a gadfly like you."

Anyone who has ever worked in a bureaucratic context knows that the above speculations are not idle. "Open doors" have a way of slamming shut on one's fingers. It is an occupational hazard. Thus, proposals are routinely made to strengthen internal dissent procedures by taking them out of the control of the people who have the power to affect employees' lives for better or for worse. Supposedly, mechanisms like internal review boards and ombudsmen "allow for criticism with much less need for heroics."[36] Not only is it usually easier to confront a stranger or disinterested party with one's worst suspicions, it is sometimes easier for these "distanced" persons to gain perspective on a situation—to figure out, for example, if a false alarm is being sounded. Nevertheless, internal review boards and ombudsmen have their own problems. They are easily co-opted and relatively powerless. When co-opted, they are used to soothe dissenters: "Don't worry, it's not really that bad."

Or they are used to exhaust dissenters. After all, one can jump through only so many bureaucratic hoops before one's will to go on dies. Even when an internal review board or ombudsman's office resists co-optation, however, it is likely to be relatively powerless; and the powerless outsider is likely to spend quiet afternoons in his or her office. Why waste time and energy "telling all" to an outsider if he or she can't really help.

For all the above reasons, the dissenter may rapidly exhaust all avenues of internal dissent. When this happens, resignation, a ritual that warns one and all that something is "rotten in Denmark," is the preferred course of action for dissenting policy experts. So powerful is resignation as a statement, that it is sometimes the only form of protest necessary. Provided that the public is suffciently upset by a resignation or a series of resignations, they will begin to ask pointed questions. Of course, if the public is neither sufficiently upset nor sufficiently curious, the protesting experts will have to make public all of the reasons for their resignation. The psychological advantage of resignation is that it helps policy experts extricate themselves from a moral bind: Should I remain loyal to my policymaking client or should I warn one or more third parties about the harm(s) likely to befall them? If I resign my position, I will be released from most of, if not all, my obligations of loyalty. So freed, I can warn my imperiled fellow citizens without suffering unnecessary pangs of guilt.

Of course, as scientist Richard Garwin (who, against President Nixon's wishes, went public on the SST issue) reminds us, the problem is not always "simply one of resignation."[37] Sometimes policy experts best serve the national good by staying on the job, either waiting for the appropriate moment to blow the whistle or continually leaking information to those most likely to be harmed. Whereas resignation (followed by protest) is the appropriate strategy if the harm risked by remaining silent is greater than the harm risked by going public, but not so great that it poses an immediate and serious threat to the people, whistle blowing is the necessary remedy if the harm at stake does in fact constitute an immediate and serious threat to the public. Before policy experts blow the whistle, Sissela Bok asks them to make sure that they are not jumping to hasty conclusions.[38] Her main reason for advising caution is that it *is* disloyal for an "insider," as well as a waste of time, to call his team the worst names first.[39]

Even though Bok has some reservations about whistle blowing, they are not nearly as great as her objections to leaking. She prefers the ways in which whistle-blowers openly accept responsibility for their tootings to the ways in which leakers hide themselves under bushel baskets.[40] In order to appreciate Bok's point, we need but consider a recent debate between social commentator Theodore Draper and Secretary of Defense Casper Weinberger. When one of Secretary Weinberger's policy experts—presumably a high-ranking science adviser—leaked passages from Weinberger's top secret "Defense Guidance" documents, Weinberger became irate. His irritation was due not only to the fact that confidentiality about a defense secret had been broken, but also to the fact that he, Weinberger, was exposed as somewhat two-faced. Apparently, Weinberger's "Defense Guidance" documents outlined plans for America to stay in a protracted nuclear war and to win it, despite the fact that he publicly assured Americans that there are no "winners" in a nuclear war.[41] In an open letter to *The New York Review of Books*, Theodore Draper told Weinberger that he should be blessing rather than cursing the leaker on his staff:

> These leaks to which you object are the very stuff of democratic policymaking. The present system of secrecy is designed to put across a new nuclear war policy as a *fait accompli*. The policy originates in the Pentagon as Secret, goes to the National Security Council as Secret, and is expected to be approved by the President as Secret.
> Why all the secrecy? The passages in your "Defense Guidance" about prevailing in a protracted nuclear war are purely political in nature, not technical. It is one thing to classify as Secret on how to make a cruise missile, it is another thing to put the same classification on a document that should be open to the most searching public discussion. . . .[42]

Although I think Draper is right to condemn the cult of secrecy, like Bok I am not so certain that leaking is the very "stuff" of democratic policymaking. First, leaking is not solely nor even mainly the province of the dissident. On the contrary, it is also a political instrument routinely wielded by policymakers and even policy experts to influence a decision, to promote policy, to persuade Congress, and to signal forign governments. According to *New York Times* correspondent Richard Halloran, leaking is used, for example, by presidential aides who are afraid to confront the President directly with bad news, by Cabinet officers who can not get past the White House palace guard to the President, and by top officials who want to convince the President to adopt their pet policies.[43] If Halloran is right, Weinberger's "leaker" may actually be Weinberger's plant. After all, one way of keeping the Russians on guard is by confusing them: Does or does not Washington believe that a nuclear war is winnable? Second, even if leaking were the province of the dissident, mere dissidence is not a license for disclosing information that could, say imperil national security. Unlike the policy expert who either resigns or whistle-blows, the policy expert who leads remains anonymous. Because the leaker's identity is a secret, it is more difficult to check his sources for accuracy and to stop him when he is serving not the best interests of the people but his own idiosyncratic causes.

CONCLUSION

This last point brings us to the conclusion of this chapter and to a shift in focus. We have noted that policy analyzing and advising will not be as responsible and as responsive as it should be unless it is bolstered by open structures and unless policy experts reconceive their role and their obligations, realizing that their ultimate client is the people and that their obligation to the people is threefold: to bring to public attention government policies or practices that they believe may threaten the public health and welfare, to speak out when they believe that public debate is being needlessly hampered by the misrepresentation or suppression of information, and to share their information with as many citizens as they practically can when public debate is not as well informed as it could be.

Admittedly, this places a burden upon those in the know, but knowledge seems to have its own imperatives; it demands to be communicated. To treat knowledge as some sort of commodity, to parcel it out to the highest bidder, is to violate the nature of knowledge. If I eat your cheese sandwich, then you are deprived of it. But it is otherwise with knowledge. If I read your article, then I am enriched and your knowledge is in no way diminished; in fact, if I respond to your article with comments and criticisms, your knowledge may be increased. On the other hand, if you fail or refuse to let me read your article, then I am deprived, and although your knowledge is in no way diminished, it cannot be increased—at least not by me. Certainly, it is sometimes justifiable not to share material things when there are not enough of them to go around. But there does not seem any reason to deny citizens access to a nondivisible good like knowledge, unless such access either threatens the public health and welfare or needlessly confuses public debate. In the absence of either of these two conditions, however, knowledge not only may but should be disseminated to as many citizens as possible. Any other policy impedes personal autonomy as well as social progress, for without knowledge, neither individuals nor communities develop.

But if we citizens refuse to listen, if we no longer care to learn, or if we are unable to understand, then there is little point to anyone disseminating information. Despite the efforts of concerned groups of citizens to get a handle on the complicated issues that pull and tear at the fabric of our existence, there is a growing tendency among us to leave things to the experts rather than to learn from the experts— and this for two interrelated reasons. In the first place, the more we know about ourselves and the more we know what we don't know about others and the world, the less in charge we seem. As our sophistication grows about the sociology of knowledge, about unconscious motivation, about propaganda techniques—in short, about the causal sources of our standards—it becomes more and more difficult for us to take a stand or to express an opinion. We debunk our own judgments before they are uttered, perhaps before they are even thought. We lapse into silence. And as our realization grows about the breadth and depth of knowledge, about fields and subfields, about multiple readings and divergent interpretations, it becomes more and more difficult for us to regard ourselves as authorities. Secondly, and relatedly, mistrusting ourselves, we respond all too quickly to those who do speak authoritatively. Out of exhaustion or frustration, we leave things to the experts, hoping that they will infuse this irrational world with rationality, much as the priests of old promised to infuse a chaotic medieval world with God's order. We want to believe that the experts' computer programs can collect our thoughts, that their cost-benefit and risk-benefit analyses can coordinate our actions, and that their word processors can codify our cacophony. And yet we know that the experts cannot deliver. Their methodologies, rational techniques, and logic are limited. Their machines, wonderful as they may be, cannot do all our thinking for us; and until they can do precisely this, we are left with the burden of being human—of playing a part in the human saga whether we want to or not.

All of us—whether President of the United States, chief science adviser, or ordinary citizen—have a role to play in the policy process. None of us is exempt, and all of us are obligated to each other through a democratic process. To the degree that we are able, we are required to take part in governing ourselves. We must do so not only because values such as justice, freedom, minority rights, and even life itself will be protected only if people are vigilant and active, but also because such participation is a form of moral self-expression. By thinking and speaking, by deciding and acting, we reaffirm that we are morally responsible persons, who have the capacity to direct the way the world goes. Says Jean Bethke Elshtain:

> One day as our children or their children or their children's children stroll in gardens, debate in public places, or poke through the ashes of a wrecked civilization, they may not rise to call us blessed. But neither will they curse our memory because we permitted, through our silence, things to pass away as in a dream.[44]

If we refuse to be silent—if we join our thoughts, words, decisions, and actions, contributing what we can to the making of public policy—our world-threatening problems may not go away. But our children won't curse us for knowingly or recklessly or negligently throwing away their inheritance, this world; indeed they may, after all and at last, bestow their benediction upon our memory.

NOTES

1. J. Nightingale, ed., *Trial of Queen Caroline*, 3 vols. (London: J. Robins & Co., Albion Press, 1820-21), vol. 2, 8.

2. E. S. Quade, *Analysis for Public Decisions*, (New York: American Elsevier Publishing Co., Inc., 1975).

3. I owe these citations to David Luban, Research Associate, Center for Philosophy and Public Policy, University of Maryland.

4. James B. Stewart, *The Partners: Inside America's Most Powerful Law Firms* (New York: Simon & Schuster, 1983), 339.

5. Ralph Nader, Peter J. Pethas, and Kate Blackwell, eds., *Whistle Blowing: The Report on the Conference on Professional Responsibility* (Indianapolis: Bobbs-Merrill Co., 1975) 9.

6. Joel Primack and Frank von Hippel, *Advice and Dissent: Scientists in the Political Arena* (New York: Basic Books, Inc., Publishers, 1974), 87-97.

7. Ibid., 91.

8. Ibid., 90.

9. Ibid., 92.

10. Ibid., 95.

11. Robert Ferber and Werner Z. Hirsch, *Social Experimentation and Economic Policy* (Cambridge, England: Cambridge University Press, 1982), 9.

12. Dennis F. Thompson, "The Denver Income Maintenance Experiment," in Amy Gutmann and Dennis Thompson, eds., *Ethics and Politics* (Chicago: Nelson-Hall Publishers, 1984), 62-74.

13. Ibid., 65.

14. Ibid., 67.

15. Ibid., 68.

16. Ibid., 67.

17. Ibid., 68.

18. Sissela Bok, *Lying: Moral Choice in Public and Private Life* (New York: Vintage Books, 1979), 198.

19. Ibid., 192.

20. Ibid.

21. Robert N. Bellah, "Social Science as Practical Reason," in Daniel Callahan and Bruce Jennings, eds., *Ethics, the Social Sciences and Policy Analysis* (New York: Plenum Press, 1983), 42–43.

22. Bruce Jennings, "Interpretive Social Science and Policy Analysis," in Callahan and Jennings, eds., *Ethics, the Social Sciences and Policy Analysis*, 34.

23. "To Tell or Not to Tell: Conflicts about Confidentiality," *Philosophy and Public Policy* 4, no. 2 (Spring 1984), 2.

24. William T. Golden, ed., *Science Advice to the President* (New York: Pergamon Press, 1980), 43.

25. U.S. Department of Defense, Office of the Director of Defense Research and Engineering, *Report of the Defense Science Board Task Force on Secrecy* (July 1, 1970), 2.

26. Sissela Bok, *Secrets* (New York: Pantheon Books, 1982).

27. Primack and von Hippel, *Advice and Dissent*, 6.

28. U.S. Atomic Energy Commission, *Underground Nuclear Testing*, AEC Report No. TID 25180 (Washington, D.C.: AEC, September 1969).

29. Dennis F. Thompson, "Bureaucracy and Democracy," in Graeme Campbell Duncan, ed., *Democratic in Theory and Practice* (New York: Cambridge University Press, 1983).

30. U.S.C.A. §52 (6) (1).

31. For typical examples, see *U.S. Federal Register* 38 (March 1, 1973), 5496 ff.

32. John H. Strange, "Citizen Participation in Community Action and Model Cities Programs," *Public Administration Review* 32 (1972), 655–59.

33. Richard L. Garwin, "Presidential Science Advising," in Golden, ed., *Science Advice to the President*, 128.

34. David W. Ewing, "The Employee's Right to Speak Out: The Management Perspective," *Civil Liberties Review* 5 (September-October 1978), 10–15.

35. Bok, *Secrets*, 226.

36. Ibid.

37. Richard L. Garwin, "Presidential Science Advising," in Golden, ed., *Science Advice to the President*, 128.

38. Bok, *Secrets*, 215.

39. Ibid., 214.

40. Ibid., 216–219.

41. Secretary of Defense Weinberger's letter of August 23, 1982, reprinted in *The New York Review of Books* 29, no. 17 (November 4, 1982), 27.

42. Theodore Draper, "Dear Mr. Weinberger: An Open Reply to an Open Letter," in ibid., 31.

43. Richard Halloran, "A Primer on the Fine Art of Leaking Information," *The New York Times*, January 14, 1983.

44. Jean Bethke Elshtain, *Public Man, Private Woman* (Princeton, N.J: Princeton University Press, 1981), 353.

Index